WHAT'S SO GREAT ABOUT AMERICA?

WHAT'S SO GREAT ABOUT AMERICA?

*LITTLE KNOWN BUT
TRUE STORIES
of FAITH, HOPE and LOVE
in AMERICA'S PAST
by*

Hal Anderson, Ph.D

Copyright © 2000 by Hal Anderson, Ph.D.

ISBN #:   Softcover   0-7388-3539-0

All rights reserved. No part of this book may be reproduced or transmitted in any form or by any means, electronic or mechanical, including photocopying, recording, or by any information storage and retrieval system, without permission in writing from the copyright owner.

This book was printed in the United States of America.

To order additional copies of this book, contact:
Xlibris Corporation
1-888-7-XLIBRIS
www.Xlibris.com
Orders@Xlibris.com

DEDICATION

We live in the most wonderfully blessed country in the world. People from around the world throughout the years have looked to America as a bastion of freedom and opportunity. The overwhelming majority of all the world's refugees seek to make their way to our shores. How thankful we should be that our forefathers, literally your grandfathers and mine, sacrificed to make America what it is.

It disturbs me that, today, the religious heritage of America is downplayed in our schools and in the media. The dedication to Christ that brought the Pilgrims to Plymouth Rock and their expression of Thanksgiving to God; the Christian beliefs of such men as John Adams, George Washington, and Benjamin Franklin, that gave them the courage to lay their lives and everything they had on the line to declare independence from the tyranny of King George; fight a Revolution against impossible odds; and author a Constitution of never before tried democratic freedom based on the Bible, is often forgotten.

After 70 years of so-called democratic socialism, based on atheism, communism proved itself an abysmal failure. America, however, after more than 200 years is still blessed with freedom, opportunity, and riches no other people in history have experienced.

I pray that we might never forget the root from whence we came—faith in the precepts of the Bible and the Christ of the Bible. It is as true today as ever, *"Unless we learn from history, we are doomed to repeat it."*

I lovingly dedicate these articles to those who were so kind as to suggest that they be gathered together into book form; to my wife, Ruth, who has been my inspiration and help for 57 years, and especially to my children and my children's children, that they might never forget the faith of their fathers.

Harold R. Anderson

SUMMARY & TABLE OF CONTENTS

1. "MULE EGGS' WON'T SATISFY (Abandonment of traditional Judeo-Christian values, held dear by America's founding fathers and for 200 years since, has not brought satisfaction and fulfilment but hopelessness, dispair & staggering social ills.) 13
2. IS AMERICA A CHRISTIAN NATION? (Patrick Henry said, "this great nation was founded not by religionists, but by Christians, not on religions, but on the gospel of Jesus Christ". Historical evidence that America is a Christian nation.) 17
3. WHAT IS CHRISTIANITY? (Historical evidence that Christ rose from the dead and is God come in the flesh to seek and to save that which is lost. Christianity is not just one way to God but the only way to God.) 21
4. THE BIBLE, A FIRM FOUNDATION (Thomas Jefferson said, "The Bible is the cornerstone of liberty". The founders of America believed the Bible to be essential to democracy and good government.) 29
5. COLUMBUS DISCOVERS AMERICA (The Christian beliefs that motivated Columbus. America was not an unspoiled paradise before Christianity came to its shores. The Aztecs practiced human sacrifice and the strong subjugated the weak.) 37
6. POCAHONTAS FINDS TRUE LOVE IN JAMESTOWN (Jamestown was founded, not only seeking material wealth, but to bring Christ to the Indians. Pocahontas was one of first converts. Only by God's providence did Jamestown survive.) 41
7. PILGRIMS SHARE THANKSGIVING WITH INDIANS (Coming to America that they might worship God without fear of persecution, the

Pilgrims, in spite of great hardship, were thankful to GOD (not the Indians) for His blessings. They shared with the Indians.) 45

8. DECLARATION OF DEPENDENCE (The Declaration of Independence was not only a declaration of independence from England, but a declaration of dependence on God. All the signers were Christians or held a Christian world view, not secular.) 49

9. AMERICA'S MIRACLE REVOLUTION (A rag-tag, ill-equipped army of patriotic Americans miraculously won independence from the most powerful nation on earth at the time. King's Mountain Men "Trusted in God and kept their powder dry.") 53

10. THE *"STAR SPANGLED BANNER "* STILL WAVES (Love of flag & country inspires great sacrifice. Francis Scott Key, composer of the "Star Spangled Banner" was a dedicated Christian.) 57

11. REVOLUTIONS THAT FAILED (Wanting the same freedoms Americans enjoyed, the French launched a Revolution based on atheism, it utterly failed. The Communist Revolution was patterned after the French. It too has proven a failure.) 61

12. GEORGE WASHINGTON, A MAN OF FAITH (George Washington, first in war, first in peace, and first in the hearts of his countrymen, known as the father of our country, was a man of prayer and great faith in the Christ he loved.) 65

13. PRAYER CHANGES THINGS AND PEOPLE (Jonathan Edwards, George Whitfield, the Great Awakening and how prayer brought the Constitution into being. Prayer meetings that influenced the course of history.) 69

14. BILL OF RIGHTS, FREEDOM *"OF"* OR *"FROM"* RELIGION (Provides a level playing field for all religions without interference from the government or a tax-supported, established church. Not intended to censor Christianity from the public sphere.) 77

15. A MISSION TO THE WORLD (St. Patrick's mission to Ireland, David Brainerd's mission to the Indians, William Carey's mission to India, the modern missionary movement and America's part in it.) 81

16. AN EDUCATED CITIZENRY NEEDED (First public schools & colleges in America founded by Christians to teach the Bible and Christian

principles. Early text books not only taught the 3 R's but Biblical values. Sunday School makes difference.) 89

17. WHAT GOD'S *"AMAZING GRACE"* CAN DO (God's "Amazing Grace" transforms lost sinners and the very ordinary into forgiven saints doing extra-ordinary things. John Newton, a former slaver, transformed by God's grace, writes "Amazing Grace.") 97

18. LIBERATED WOMEN WHO MADE THEIR LIFE COUNT (A mother, Susanna Wesley, and blind Fanny Crosby inspire and influence history. Conversion of John and Charles Wesley, the Moravians, and the Wesleyan revival. Fanny Crosby writes 8,000 hymns.) 101

19. ABRAHAM LINCOLN, LOG CABIN TO MANSION (Honest Abe rises from poverty and obscurity and many failures to become President and the great emancipator. Accepted Christ as his personal Savior shortly before his assassination on a Good Friday.) 109

20. HOW THE WEST WAS WON (The Louisiana Purchase, Lewis and Clark, the Alamo, Pony Express, Teddy Roosevelt, and road builder, R.G. LeTourneau, opens the West.) 113

21. SALVATION ARMY, GOD'S GOOD SAMARITANS (William Booth founds the Salvation Army to reach the poor and needy with the gospel by ministering first to their physical needs. Daughter, Evangeline Booth, brings the Salvation Army to America.) 121

22. ALCOHOLIC'S ANONYMOUS & A POWER GREATER (Two alcoholic's, stock broker, Bill W. and physician, Dr. Bob, overcome their addiction through Christ, a Power greater than themselves. They found Alcoholic's Anonymous and the 12 step program.) 125

23. WAR TO END ALL WARS (World War I did not end all wars. Although man keeps trying through "globalism" and his own efforts to bring peace to a sinful world, only the "Prince of Peace" can and will bring lasting peace. 130

24. WHY HITLER STARTED A HOLOCAUST (Hitler's belief in the occult and atheist, Friedrich Nietzsche's philosophy, that only the fittest should survive as taught by evolution. Many Christians, Corrie Ten Boom, and others, however, helped the Jews.) 134

25. PEARL HARBOR, THE ATOM BOMB & WORLD WAR II (World War II miracles: "D" Day; Doolittle's raid on Tokyo and Jacob de Shazer.

Pearl Harbor bomber pilot, Commander, Mitsuo Fuchida becomes Christian.) 138

26. MAN'S JUSTICE BRINGS GOD'S MERCY (During the War Crimes Trial, following WW II, Chaplain Henry Gerecke shares Christ with Hitler's elite, Goering, Keitel, Ribbentrop and others.) 146

27. BILLY GRAHAM, EVANGELIST TO THE WORLD (Stuart Hamblen accepts Christ, Hearst "puffs" Graham, and "Billy" becomes evangelist to the world, winning millions to Christ. He is spirtual advisor to Presidents, and one of America's most admired men.) 150

28. ELVIS STILL LIVES IN ROCK 'N' ROLL (Elvis has been worshiped by a generation as "the King", but his step-brother, Rick Stanley, worships the King of Kings and preaches the gospel.) 154

29. DRUGS, ROCK 'N' ROLL & THE JESUS REVOLUTION (The "Jesus Revolution" becomes world wide news as former drug addicted "Hippies" find deliverance and meaning through Christ.) 158

30. ASTRONAUTS IN SPACE FEEL GOD'S PRESENCE (American flag and Bible planted on the Moon. Testimonies of astronauts, James Irwin, Frank Borman, Jack Lousma and others of the Creator's presence in space.) 162

31. EVOLUTION, IS IT FACT OR FAITH? (Evolution not a proven scientific fact but a religion. Enables the "devotee" to avoid accountability to a Creator God in spite of evidence to the contrary. If evolution is fact, Christ is not God and our Savior.) 166

32. LAND OF OPPORTUNITY AND THE SECOND CHANCE (Refugees from persecution and poverty in other lands have found in America the freedom to succeed or fail. The Statue of Liberty stands as a symbol of the American Dream and the "Protestant work ethic".) 174

33. WHATEVER HAPPENED TO SIN? (Moral Relativism, Self-Esteemism and Victimism makes man his own god. B. J. Thomas finds self-worth in Christ. Chuck Colson is "Born Again" and finds forgiveness of sin through Christ.) 182

34. WHATEVER HAPPENED TO AMERICA'S SCHOOLS? (The religion of secular humanism holds hostage the public school. William Murray, son of atheist, Madalyn Murray O'Hair, who sued to have the Bible and Prayer outlawed in public school, finds Christ.) 190

35. WHATEVER HAPPENED TO THE FAMILY? (The traditional family has become the fractured family in America. God established the home when He created Adam and Eve. It is held together by commitment and unconditional love, which is a choice.) 198
36. SATISFACTION GUARANTEED, NOW AND FOREVER (Dale Evans and Roy Rogers find true satisfaction not in fame and fortune, but in Christ. Nicky Cruz finds satisfaction and deliverance from drugs and gangs through Christian love.) 206

FOREWORD

It has been my distinct privilege to know and work with Pastor Harold R. Anderson since 1992. This gentle man of faith has a boundless love for humanity and an extraordinary way of weaving truth, morality, hope, love, faith and historical occurrences into his sermons and articles. Through his strong interest in the history of our country, he has uncovered many interesting and little-known incidents which he uses to focus the readers' attention not only on the issues of the past but also on those which remain with us today.

What's So Great About America? is a collection of Pastor Anderson's work which best exemplifies the spirit of America, which we many times feel no longer exists. Anderson's optimistic view that there is some good in everyone is a refreshing change from stories seen in the daily newspapers, radio and television broadcasts and on the silver screen where the most ghastly horrors man can commit receive top billing.

Pastor Anderson served under General George Patton in World War II and has an abiding love for his country. He firmly believes that the basic religious concepts on which the United States of America were founded should be retained in our government and also returned to our nation's schools and to the media.

What's So Great About Anierica? According to Pastor Anderson, it is the faith. hope and love which has existed in this country since before it became a nation. Only time will tell whether the "great experiment" known as the United States of America will survive the problems it faces now and in the future. But it has been a noble experiment. One in which Pastor Anderson has high hopes will prevail if the people return religious principles to their prominence at the time of our country's founding.

William E. Ewing
Former Editor *The Leader*
Lucerne Valley, CA.

CHAPTER 1

"MULE EGGS" WON'T SATISFY

I once heard about two city slickers, who had spent their whole lives in the city. They grew tired of the congestion of the city, however, and decided they wanted to move out into the country. They had just about *"had it"* with urban living. They bought a ranch in the country and decided they were going to live off the land, just like their ancestors.

One of them remembered how his grandpa used to talk about having a mule. So, the first thing they decided they needed in order to ranch was a mule. They went to a neighboring rancher and asked him if he had a mule to sell. The rancher, surprised by the request, replied, *"No, I'm afraid not."*

They were disappointed, but decided to stand around and visit with the rancher for a few moments. One of them saw some watermelons stacked against the barn and asked the rancher, *"What are those?"*

The rancher, seeing that these two were hopeless city slickers, decided to have some fun. *"Oh,"* he answered, *"Those are mule eggs." "You take one of those eggs home and wait for it to hatch and you'll have a mule.* The city slickers were overjoyed and offered to buy one of those *"mule eggs."* They agreed on a fair price, put one of those watermelons in the back of their pick-up, and headed down the bumpy country road toward their own ranch.

Suddenly they hit a big bump in the road and the watermelon bounced out of the truck, hit the road, and burst open. Seeing in his rearview mirror what had happened, the driver hurriedly turned his truck around and drove back to retrieve his *"mule egg.* A big old jackrabbit happened to be hopping by right then, saw the watermelon and hopped over to it. Standing in the middle of that watermelon, he begins to eat.

Here comes the two city slickers. They spy their *"mule egg"* burst open, and there is this long-eared creature in the middle of it. One of the men shouts, *"Our mule egg has hatched!!* Seeing those two men coming toward it, the jack rabbit takes off, with the two men in hot pursuit. Finally, they could go no farther. Both men fell wearily onto the ground, gasping for air, while the jack rabbit hopped off into the distance.

Raising up on his elbow, one of the men said, *"Well, I guess we lost our mule."* The other nodded grimly, *"Yes, but you know,"* he said, *"I'm not sure I wanted to plow that fast anyway."*

One of the problems with getting old is, that *even though you may want to plow as fast as ever, you just can't. The spirit may be willing, but the flesh is weak.* Things are moving so fast these days, its almost impossible even for the young to keep up with all the new things that are constantly rushing in upon us. Too often, we tend to think that if something is *"new"* it must be *"better"* than the *"old"*. But that *"ain't"* necessarily so.

One thing about growing old, you discover that there are a lot of *"MULE EGGS"* out there, that you may have *put* your faith and hope in, but they *disappointed* you and *failed to satisfy.*

Many people become alarmed when they first discover their hair is turning gray, or they're getting wrinkles. But, really, these marks of age should be worn as a badge of honor. It shows that *"we have been around the block a few times"* and *"been there"* and *"done that"*. Because of the tremendous *"new"* advances made in the science of medicine in recent years, there are more of us *"old codgers"* (Senior Citizens) today, than ever before, and we produced a bumper crop of babies after World War II. Now, these young *"whipper snappers"* (Baby Boomers) are running things.

"Oh God, help us old folks to be patient with them. Help them, Lord, to learn from the mistakes we made. They, too, are concerned,

now, about growing old. Help us all to learn to grow old, if not gracefully, at least, grateful for our blessings."

America, too, as a sovereign nation is growing old. It is over two centuries old and well into the third century. And while other attempts at democracy have come and gone, American democracy still lives. We ask the question, *"Why has America's experiment in democracy (the first of its kind in history), survived, while others have fallen by the way side?"*

One of the world's most respected and honored historians, Arnold Toynbee, is quoted as having said, *"No republic has existed longer than 200 years whose mind and will is not entwined around the will of God."*

With the increasing denial of any place for God, the Bible and prayer in public life, in the name of *Separation of Church and State* and *"political correctness"*, and the scraping of the *traditional Judeo-Christian values* held dear by America's founding fathers, and for 200 years since, *we wonder how long America has.* A *"New World Order"*, a *"New Age"* religion, and a *"New Morality"* has become the fashion of the day.

Generations born after World War II grew up hearing how happiness was theirs to *grab*. Drugs promised *higher consciousness* and the sexual revolution promised *freedom* from the shackles of out-dated *concepts* of right and wrong. *"If it feels good, do it,"* became the watchword. They were going to have it all, or at least have a great time trying. So, they *showed up* at *life's buffet*, assuming their *plates* would be *filled*. Maybe their Depression-era parents and grandparents were satisfied just to have food on the table, but things were *different now*. *The bluebird of happiness was just around the corner.*

Something, however, *went* terribly *wrong* on the way to the *"feel good"* cafeteria. An Associated Press poll indicates that *"baby boomers"* are *four times likelier* to *say* they're *not satisfied* with their lives than are people of their *parents' generation*. Experts estimate the incidence of *psychological depression* is *10 times* what it was *pre-World*

War II, even *though* America has experienced an unprecedented period of *economic prosperity* since.

Drugs, alcohol and promiscuous sex have proven to be killers. AIDS and other venereal diseases are epidemic. Half of all marriages end in divorce, and overwhelming numbers of America's children are being raised in single parent homes. Teen age gangs make our city streets *killing fields*. Kids are killing kids in our public schools, as the Ten Commandments have been removed from any display on the walls, lest, as the court says, *"...impressionable children might see them and be influenced by them".*

The same courts refuse to believe that children might be influenced by the violence and sex portrayed so often and so graphically on TV, and in the movies. Their ears are bombarded with *"Rock" lyrics* that often promote drugs, violence, and sexual promiscuity. *Perhaps someone should inform those companies that spend millions of dollars for 30 second commercials on TV, to influence people to buy their products, that they're wasting their money, if TV doesn't influence behavior.*

The illusive *"brass ring"* of *"happiness and feeling good"* has escaped the grasp of overwhelming numbers swept along in the river of dispair and disappointment. Billions of taxpayer dollars have been spent in rescue attempts, but things only seem to get worse. *Perhaps it's time we did something about the cause.*

The foundation upon which America was built has crumbled beneath the load, as we have little by little chipped it away, believing it to be *too hopelessly old fashioned* for this day and age of *"enlightenment"*. What was that foundation upon which America was built?

Noah Webster, who fought in the American Revolution and produced the first Dictionary, said it best, *"The moral principles and precepts contained in the Scriptures ought to form the basis of all our civil constitutions and laws. All the miseries and evils which men suffer from vice, crime, injustice, oppression, slavery, and war, proceed from their despising or neglecting the precepts contained in the Bible...The religion which has introduced civil liberty is the religion of Christ...to this we owe our free constitutions of government."*

CHAPTER 2

IS AMERICA A CHRISTIAN NATION?

When Mississippi Governor, Kirk Fordice, remarked that *"America is a Christian nation,"* he drew near hysterical opposition. His opponents, however, spoke from emotion, not historical fact. Christianity has been the basis not only of our legal system, but of our culture as well.

Some of the current anti-Christian bias comes from a misunderstanding of what is meant by the term *"Christian nation."* The term does not presume that everyone is now or was a Christian, nor that everyone lives as a Christian should. Neither does it mean that people should be forced to profess Christianity. Non-Christians are not denied the freedom to express opinions contrary to the Christian consensus.

References to our Christian roots may be found as recently as the last generation. President Franklin Roosevelt described the United States as *"founded on the principles of Christianity,"* and President Truman wrote, *"This is a Christian nation".*

Patrick Henry said, *"It cannot be emphasized too strongly or too often that this great nation was founded, not by religionists, but by Christians; not on religions, but on the gospel of Jesus Christ."* John Quincy Adams wrote, *"The highest glory of the American Revolution was this, it connected in one indissoluble bond, the principles of civil government with the principles of Christianity."*

A landmark decision handed down by the United States Supreme Court in 1892, states:*"Our laws and our institutions must necessarily be based upon and embody the teachings of the Redeemer of mankind. It is impossible that it should be otherwise; and in this sense and to this extent our civilization and our institutions are emphatically Christian... This is a religious people. This is historically true. From the discovery of this continent to the present hour, there is a single voice making this affirmation...we find everywhere a clear recognition of the same truth... These, and many other matters which might be noticed, add a volume of unofficial declarations to the mass of organic utterances that this is a Christian nation."* (Church of the Holy Trinity v. United States.)

America is a miracle nation. It was a miracle that Columbus found this part of the world. It was a miracle that the early colonists survived and built a nation during those first 156 years. It was a miracle that they rebelled against the motherland, and even a greater miracle that they won the Revolutionary War against overwhelming odds. It was a miracle that they founded upon this continent a new nation dedicated to the proposition that all men are created equal, *"—equal under God, and equal before the law."* It was a miracle that 13 independent states could agree on a national constitution. It is a miracle that this nation exists today through a civil war, a devastating depression, and two world wars. Yet, today, America is the nation to which most of the world's refugees and immigrants want to come.

At the time the *Constitution* and the *Bill of Rights* was written, (1787-89), two dominant philosophies prevailed in the western world. One was religious, the other secular. Those with a religious world view based their entire philosophy upon a belief in God as creator and sustainer of the universe. Everything else flowed from that premise.

They believed man was a created being, responsible to God to obey the truths He revealed for humanity in the Bible. The secularists, including *atheists, skeptics, rationalists,* and others of the so-called *Enlightenment,* began their philosophy without God. To the secularist, all of life—*humanity, morals, education, and science*—*must be considered without God.*

In recent years, some have claimed that the Fathers of our

country were not Christians or religious people, but secularists. *Nothing could be further from the truth.* Of the 55 men who wrote and signed the U. S. Constitution, 50 of the 55 were members of one of the various Protestant denominations. Two were Catholic. Three belonged to no church, *but* held a Christian world view.

So religious was the climate in America *when* the *Constitution* and the *Bill of Rights* was framed, that Benjamin Franklin, while Ambassador in Europe, in his pamphlet, *"Information to Those Who Would Remove to America",* wrote: *"...bad examples to youth are rare in America, which must be a comfortable consideration to parents.... serious religion, under its various denominations, is not only tolerated but respected and practiced. Atheism is unknown there; Infidelity rare and secret; so that persons may live to a great age in that country without having their piety shocked by meeting with either an Atheist or an Infidel. And the Divine Being seems to have manifested his approbation of the mutual forbearance and kindness with which the different sects treat each other, by the remarkable prosperity with which He (God) has been pleased to favor the whole country."*

Franklin, who didn't believe this nation to be founded or populated by infidels, atheists, or secularists, was obviously a greater authority on conditions in early America than modern secularizers. America was established largely by immigrants from nothern Europe, the area most influenced by the Reformation. It was founded by *"rugged individualists", "dissenters"* who came to these shores to escape persecution of a State controlled church and to have the freedom to worship God and His Son, Jesus Christ, as they interpreted the *"Holy Scriptures"* without fear of molestation.

Pollster, George Gallup, has stated, *"Christianity is the predominant religious affiliation professed by Americans; our culture and even our laws reflect it."*

This was borne out in a recent survey by the City University of New York. It was found that 86% of Americans claim to be Christian. (*60% Protestant, 26% Catholic*). Only 7.5% said they had no religious preference. Of the remainder, 2% were Jewish, and

4% all other religions. Muslims listed only 0.5%, and most Asian Americans are not Buddhist, Hindu, or Muslim, but Christian.

In his message to the 76th Congress, President Franklin Roosevelt, who led us through World War II, said: *"Storms from abroad directly challenge three institutions indispensable to Americans now as always. The first is religion, and is the source of the other two—democracy and international good faith. Religion, by teaching man his relationship to God, gives the individual a sense of his own dignity and teaches him to respect himself by respecting his neighbors. Where freedom of religion has been attacked, the attack has come from sources opposed to democracy."*

Professor Harvey Cox of Harvard University made the following observation, *"Secularism is not only indifferent to alternative religious systems, but as a religious ideology, it is opposed to any other religious systems..."* Moreover he says, *"Secularism is a dangerous ideological system because it seeks to impose its ideology through the organs of the State. Because secularism has little or no tolerance and is opposed to other religions, it actively rejects, excludes and attempts to eliminate Christianity from meaningful participation in society..."*

French philosopher and sociologist, Alex DeTocqueville visited America in her infancy to find the secret of her greatness. As he traveled from town to town, he talked with people and asked questions. He examined America's schools and centers of business, but could not find in them the reason for our strength. Not until he visited the churches of America and witnessed the pulpits of the land, *"aflame with righteousness"* did he find the secret of America's greatness. Returning to France, he summarized his findings: *"Amerca is great because America is good; and if America ever ceases to be good, America will cease to be great."*

CHAPTER 3

WHAT IS CHRISTIANITY?

Ed and Fred caught more fish on their first time out than some do in a lifetime. Before heading back to the boat rental, they talked about trying to mark the place of their good fortune.

They assumed that if they could find this *"hot spot"* again, they would be able to relive their success. So Ed pulled out a jackknife and carved a notch in the boat at the exact place they had been casting their lines.

When Fred looked over and saw Ed marking the spot, he couldn't believe his eyes. *"Don't be stupid, Ed!"*, he growled. *"That won't do any good. What if we get a different boat?"*

Ed and Fred were both sincere in their reasoning. But their sincerity would never bring them back to the place they wanted to be. *It's easy to be completely sincere, and yet be badly mistaken!*

A physician was administering a mixture of oxygen and anesthetic gas to a patient in a New York hospital. When one of the tanks was empty, the doctor used a new one marked Oxygen. Almost immediately the patient died.

The coroner's autopsy revealed carbon dioxide poisoning. Upon investigation the second tank was found to contain pure CO_2, and had somehow been mislabeled.

The doctor had no doubt that he was using oxygen, when he administered the lethal gas. No one wanted the tragedy to happen, yet they were all sincerely wrong. Likewise, in the matter of religion and salvation, many say, *"It really doesn't make any differ-*

ence what I believe, as long as I am sincere, I'll come out all right in the end."

Tom and Stephen were discussing *the meaning of life.* Tom said, *"I don't see any difference between the world religions. They teach basically the same things; they believe in a supreme being, they speak of an afterlife, they present us with ethical guidelines for living, and they tell us about great religious leaders who lived exemplary lives. It's kind of like shopping around for the religion that fits you."*

Stephen replied, *"But I think you've left out one very important point." "What's that?"* Tom responded.

"The law of non-contradiction says that if I say your sweater is all white, and you say your sweater is all black, we can't both be right. Either you are right, or I am right, or we are both wrong. We can't both be right at the same time."

"So how does that affect my argument?" Tom retorted. *"Well, you say that all the world religions are the same, and yet they teach very different things."*

"Look at the five major world religions: Islam, Judaism, Christianity, Hinduism, and Buddhism. Each has a radically different view of God; they talk about very different kinds of afterlives; they teach different things about ethics; and they teach different things about the origin of man. So, either all religions are wrong, or one is right, but they cannot all be right at the same time ."

It is popular, today, to claim that all the world religions are true and that none of them are wrong. Yet this contention violates logic.

Christianity is fundamentally different from all the other world religions, because of its founder, *Jesus Christ.* Jesus is the only religious leader who makes the claim that He is the one, true, creator God. Jesus said, *"I am the way, the truth, and the life: no man cometh unto the Father, but by Me."* (John 14:6)

Muhammad, Buddha, Krishna, and Confucius all affirmed that they were mere men. None dared claim to be God. Yet Jesus said that he possessed the very nature of God. In John 10:30-33, Jesus said, *"I and the Father are one."* By this he meant that he and the

Father were one in essence. Jesus, also said, *"He that has seen me, hath seen the Father."* (Jn. 14:9)

Immediately after Jesus said this, the people took up stones to kill him for blasphemy. They realized he was claiming to be God. Jesus could have saved himself from the agonizing torture of crucifixion had He renounced His claim to be God.

C. S. Lewis, world reknowned, British author and professor at Cambridge University, was an agnostic until he examined the evidence. He thoroughly examined all the world's religions with the presuposition that there was good to be found in all, and that Jesus was nothing more than a great moral teacher. His research, however, led to his conversion to Christianity. He wrote in *"Mere Christianity"*, concerning Jesus:

"A man who was merely a man and said the sort of things Jesus said would not be a great moral teacher. He would either be a lunatic—on a level with the man who says he is a poached egg—or else he would be the Devil of Hell.

You must make your choice. Either this man was, and is, the Son of God: or else a madman or something worse. You can shut Him up for a fool, you can spit at Him and kill Him as demon; or you can fall at His feet and call Him Lord and God. But let us not come with any patronizing nonsense about His being a great human teacher. He has not left that open to us. He did not intend to."

There are only a few major world religions that are based on personalities instead of a philosophical system, and only Christianity claims an empty tomb for its founder.

The resurrection of Christ is the most profound and basic tenet of Christianity. It is the historical FACT on which Christianity is built. The apostle Paul says, *"...If Christ has not been raised, your faith is futile;...If only for this life we have hope in Christ, we are to be pitied more than all men."* (I Cor. 15:17-19)

Josephus, not a Christian, but a highly respected Jewish historian, wrote at the end of the first century A.D. an amazing passage in his *"Antiquities"*: *"Now there was about this time Jesus, a wise man, if it be lawful to call him a man; for he was a doer of wonderful works,...This man was the Christ. And when Pilate had condemned him to the cross, upon his impeachment by the principle men among us; those who had loved him from the first did not forsake him, for he appeared to them alive on the third day..."* It is a matter of history that the apostles from the very beginning made many converts in Jerusalem, hostile as it was, by proclaiming the glad news that Christ had risen from the grave—and they did it within a short walk from the sepulchre. Any one of their hearers could have visited the tomb and come back again in a few short minutes. Is it conceivable, that the apostles would have had such success winning followers, if the body of the one they proclaimed as risen, was all the time decomposing in that borrowed tomb?

In a book which has become a best-seller, *"Who Moved the Stone?"* Frank Morrison, a lawyer and journalist, tells how he had been brought up in a rationalistic environment. He had believed that the resurrection of Jesus Christ was nothing but a fairy tale happy ending.

Therefore, he planned to write an account of the last tragic days of Jesus, omitting, of course, any suspicion of the miraculous, and would utterly discount the resurrection. But, alas, when he came to study the historical facts with his legal training and applying the laws of evidence, he had to change his mind. He wrote his book instead, confirming that the miraculous resurrection of Christ was an indisputable fact of history. His first chapter is significantly called, *"The Book that Refused to Be Written".*

Morrison discovered that Christ was publicly put in the tomb on Friday, but on Sunday morning the body was missing. If He did not rise from the dead, then someone took the body; the Romans, the Jews or the disciples.

The Romans would have had no reason to steal the body, since they wanted to keep the peace in Palestine. The idea was to keep the provinces as quiet as possible, and stealing the body of Christ would not accomplish this objective. They would have broken their own law, for the seal of Rome sealed the tomb.

The Jews would not have taken the body, because the last

thing they wanted was a proclamation of the resurrection. They were the ones who asked for the guard. To break the seal of Rome would have started a holocaust.

The disciples of Jesus had no reason to steal the body, and if they did, they later died for something they knew to be untrue. Surely in the face of excruciating torture and death for preaching what they knew to be a lie, someone would have broken down and confessed that they had conspired to deceive the world by stealing the body. Without exception, however, they all continued to proclaim, *"Christ is risen!"*

When the disciples of Jesus proclaimed the resurrection, they did so as eyewitnesses and they did so while people were still alive who had had contact with the events they spoke of. In 56 A.D. Paul wrote that over 500 people had seen the risen Jesus and that most of them were still alive. It passes the bounds of credibility that the early Christians could have manufactured such a tale and then preached it among those who might easily have refuted it simply by producing the body of Jesus.

Only the miraculous resurrection of Jesus can account for the astonishing change in the lives of the disciples in so short a time. Think of the psychological absurdity of a little band of defeated cowards cowering in an upper room one day and a few days later transformed into a company that no persecution could silence—and then attempting to attribute this dramatic change to nothing more convincing than a miserable fabrication they were trying to foist upon the world.

Dr. Simon Greenleaf, according to the *"Dictionary of American Biography"*, was one of the greatest legal minds America has produced. He was one of the founders of Harvard Law School and helped bring it to its position of prominence today. Greenleaf wrote a volume in which he examined the legal value of the apostles' testimony to the resurrection of Christ. He put each in turn on the witness stand. *He concluded that the resurrection of Christ was one of the best supported events in all of history, according to the laws of legal evidence that might be administered in a court of justice.*

Dr. Thomas Arnold, author of a famous three-volume *"History of Rome"*, and professor of history at Oxford, wrote, *"I know of no one FACT in the history of mankind which is proved by better and fuller evidence of every sort, to the understanding of a FAIR inquirer, than...that Christ died and rose again from the dead."*

Christianity began with one penniless, homeless preacher from a peasant family in a small insignificant village in a tiny subjugated country in the Roman Empire. He was rejected by his own people, tried and put to death as a criminal. And yet today his followers number in the billions.

How did the early Christian church survive? Humanly speaking, the odds were all stacked against it. It was unthinkable that a small, despised movement from a corner of Palestine could move out to become the dominant faith of the mighty Roman Empire, an empire steeped in fiercely defended traditional pagan religions.

Christianity was considered an illegal and depraved religion. Wave after wave of persecution was unleashed to squash it. All but one of the apostles of Jesus suffered a martyr's death.

Tired of having to look out on the poverty that surrounded the palace, Nero devised a *slum clearance program*. He set fire to the houses of the slum dwellers, but the fire got out of hand and destroyed most of Rome.

The ancient Roman historian, Tacitus, describes what happened as a result. *"Therefore to scotch the rumor (of his starting the fire), Nero substituted as culprits, and punished with the utmost refinements of cruelty a class of men...whom the crowd styled Christians."*

We picture the Colosseum of Rome filled to overflowing. The crowd roars. They want entertainment. Christians by the hundreds are spread across the arena. Nero is outraged, for rather than begging for mercy, renouncing their Christ, or running in terror, these hated Christians sing hymns to their God. Peace seems to radiate from their faces. Nero can't stand it. Finally he gives the thumbs down sign for the spectacle of death to begin.

Huge iron gates into the arena open as scores of hungry, purposely starved lions, leap into the stadium. While still singing, with their faces turned toward heaven, the Christians are pounced upon by the hungry lions and their bodies ripped and torn by tooth and claw. As the crowd views the bloody spectacle, they roar their approval. Their god, Nero, the Roman Emperor, has again provided a circus for their entertainment.

Why were the early Christians willing to bear unspeakable torture and death rather than worship the Roman emperor and sacrifice to the gods of Rome? Why were they so stubborn? How easy it would have been to be broadminded and agree with the prevailing attitude of the day, that there were many gods and their Christ was only one among many.

In spite of the persecution Christians have faced throughout the centuries for their narrow-mindedness, there is one thing those that have experienced Christ agree on, and that is that Jesus is God and the only true God.

The earliest Christians did not have church buildings. They typically met in homes. They had no access to the mass media of their day. So how can we account for their rapid expansion until by the time of Emperor Constantine, (313 A.D.) half of the civilized world professed Christianity.

In the urban areas the people lived close together in crowded tenements. There were few secrets in such a setting. The faith spread as neighbors saw the lives of the believers close-up, on a daily basis.

And what kind of lives did they lead? Justin Martyr, a noted early Christian theologian, wrote to Emperor Antoninus Pius and described the believers: *"We formerly rejoiced in uncleanness of life, but now love only chastity; before we used the magic arts, but now dedicate ourselves to the true and unbegotten God; before we loved money and possessions more than anything, but now we share what we have and to everyone who is in need; before we hated one another and killed one another and would not eat with those of another race, but now since the manifestation of Christ, we have come to a common life and pray for our enemies and try to win over those who hate us without just cause."*

When Emperor Julian *"the Apostate"* wanted to revive pagan religion in the mid-300s, he gave a most helpful insight into how the church spread. This opponent of the faith said that Christianity *"has been specially advanced through the loving service rendered to strangers...the Christians care not only for their own poor but for ours as well; while those who belong to us look in vain for the help we should render them."*

On the surface, the early Christians appeared powerless and weak, they were an easy target for scorn and ridicule. They had no great financial resources, no buildings, no social status, no government approval, no respect from the educators. But what finally mattered is what they did have—a living faith in a risen Savior.

They had a loving fellowship with one another. They had a new way of life that gave them joy and peace in the midst of the storms. *They were new creatures in Christ Jesus.*

Polycarp at 86 was pastor of the church in Smyrna, which is mentioned in the Book of Revelation He was a personal friend and pupil of John the Apostle. He was thrown in prison for preaching. He was urged by the Roman proconsul to denounce Christ and he would be set free.

Polycarp replied, *"Eighty and six years have I served my Lord, and He never did me any injury. How then can I blaspheme my King and my Saviour?"* He was tied to a stake and with flames lapping at his body, Polycarp died with a smile on his face, singing the praises of the Christ he loved.

CHAPTER 4

THE BIBLE, A FIRM FOUNDATION

No other book in history has been held in such high esteem as has the Bible, especially in America. From the inauguration of George Washington to the present, America's Presidents have taken their oath of office with their hand upon the Bible. Witnesses in our nations courts swear to tell the truth with their hand upon the Bible.

The Bible remains the most published, most translated, most sought after book of all time. It is the world's best seller. Millions upon millions of Bibles have flooded into Communist countries, where until recently it had been banned and ridiculed.

A Book Fair was held in Moscow several years ago. The table of Christian books with the Bible was located just around the corner from Madelyn Murray O'Hare's atheistic materials. Her booth stood empty the whole time, while police had to be brought in to control the huge crowds wanting to get a Bible!

Perhaps one of the greatest contributing events in history to the eventual birth of America and its new experiment in democracy and human freedom was the invention of the printing press. In 1453 Johannes Gutenberg presented to the world the first book ever printed by moveable type, the Bible.

Until this time any books available, including the Bible, were laboriously copied by hand. Only the clergy, who did most of the copying, kings and the nobility had access to the Bible. With the invention of the printing press, however, the Bible and other books became available to the common man.

It was like opening a Pandora's box. New ideas, philosophies and theologies began to explode out to the masses, to the consternation, fear and anger of many of those that had enjoyed for centuries the privileges of control over the common people, because of the union of Church and State. Protestant Reformers put the Bible into the hands of the masses and taught them to read it and think for themselves.

Concepts of government were revolutionized and the millenium of history called the *"Dark Ages"* began to draw to a close as the light of God's *unadulterated* Word illuminated the hearts and minds of man.

The first to translate the Bible into English was William Tyndale. He was born in 1494, in Gloucester, England, just two years after Columbus discovered America. Tyndale wanted, *"every plough-boy"* to be able to read the Bible.

For his efforts, he was driven from England and finally strangled to death. So incensed were the ecclesiatical authorities at what he had dared to do, that not only did they burn every copy, that could be found, they dug up his dead body, burned it and threw the ashes in the nearby river. And yet, only a few years later, his translation was used in the main for the *"Authorized King James Version"* in 1611.

The common people read for themselves the words of Christ that *"God so loved the world that He gave His only begotten Son that whosoever (everybody regardless of position or wealth) believeth in Him should not perish but have everlasting life."* (John 3:16) and that *"God is no respecter of persons: But in every nation he that feareth Him, and worketh righteousness, is accepted with Him."* (Acts 10:34,35) and that *"ye are all the children of God by faith in Christ Jesus...There is neither Jew nor Greek, there is neither bond nor free, there is neither male nor female, for ye are all one in Christ Jesus."* (Gal. 3:26,28)

As a result America's founding fathers declared to the world their belief in a personal, infinite God—*"their Creator"*—who endowed them (*all men*) with *"certain inalienable"* or absolute rights.

"To the men of that time," says constitutional lawyer, John W.

Whitehead, *"it was self-evident that if there were no God there could be no absolute rights."*

One need only stand in the portals of the Jefferson Memorial and read Jefferson's words engraved there, to understand the founders' thoughts: *"God who gave us life gave us liberty, Can the liberties of a nation be secure when we have removed a conviction that these liberties are the gift of God?"*

America's founding fathers had not the arrogance that is so prevalent today, especially among the followers of Karl Marx and the *"Secularists"*, that by social engineering and their God-like superior wisdom, the evolution of a man-made utopia can be brought into existence without God. They knew that because of man's sinful nature, as taught in the Bible, if their new experiment in free-enterprise and Constitutional Government by the people was to suceed, they would need God's help and a lot of it.

Because of man's fallen nature, as revealed in the Bible, it was clear that man could not be his own judge—God stood in judgment—even over government. And every man was responsible for his actions to an All-seeing, All-knowing, Sovereign God. Civil government was a necessary evil and the less the better. God was their Provider, not *"Big Brother"*.

On the *"Liberty Bell"* at Independence Hall in Philadelphia is engraved a quote from the Bible, *"Proclaim Liberty throughout the land"* (Lev. 25:10).

In Washington, D.C. there is set aside in the Capitol building a small prayer room just off the rotunda. The rooms focal point is a stained glass window showing George Washington kneeling in prayer. Behind him is etched the words, *"Preserve me, O God, for in Thee do I put my trust."* (Psalm 16:1).

Above the head of the Chief Justice of the Supreme Court are the *Ten Commandments*, with the great American eagle protecting them.

Lining the walls of the stairwell of the Washington Monument are such biblical phrases as *"Search the Scriptures,"* *"Holiness* to the Lord," "*Train up a child in the way he should go, and when he is old he will not depart from it.*"

On the walls of the Library of Congress are the words, "*What doth the Lord require of thee, but to do justly and love mercy and walk humbly with thy God.*" (Micah 6:8) Another says, "*The heavens declare the glory of God, and the firmament sheweth his handiwork.*" (Psalms 19:1)

H. G. Wells, noted English novelist and author of the momentous work, "*Outline of History*", although an atheist, wrote, "*The Bible has been the Book that held together the fabric of Western civilization... The civilization we possess could not have come into existence and could not have been sustained without it.*"

William Lyon Phelps, distinguished professor of English literature at both Harvard and Yale Universities wrote, "*Everyone who has a thorough knowledge of the Bible may truly be called educated... I believe knowledge of the Bible without a college education is more valuable than a college education without the Bible.*"

Count Leo Tolstoy, Russian novelist and social reformer wrote, "*Without the Bible the education of a child in the present state of society is impossible.*"

John Locke was a physician, an educator and professor at Oxford, a noted philosopher and author. He was a leader in speaking out against the censorship of the press. He wrote concerning the Bible, "*It has God for its Author, salvation for its end, and truth, without any mixture of error, for its matter; it is all pure, sincere, nothing too much, nothing wanting.*"

Charles Dickens, who through his writings brought much needed reforms to Englands' prisons, workhouses, and schools, wrote concerning the Bible, "*It is the best Book that ever was or ever will be in the world...*"

Horace Greeley said, "*It is impossible to mentally or socially enslave a Bible-reading people. The principles of the Bible are the groundwork of human freedom.*"

Throughout the years America's Presidents have called upon

God to help them govern and emphasized the Bible as the *foundation upon which America was built.*

George Washington said, *"It is impossible rightly to govern the world without God and the Bible."*

Thomas Jefferson, writer of the Declaration of Independence and third President said, *"The Bible is the cornerstone of liberty."*

James Madison is known as the Father of the Constitution and especially the Bill of Rights. He was a member of the first congress and fourth President.

One historian, William Rives, writes in *"History of the Life and Times of James Madison"*, *"After the manner of the Bereans he seems to have searched the Scriptures daily and diligently...He explored the whole history and evidences of Christianity on every side..."*

Madison said, *"The belief in a God, All Powerful, wise and good, is so essential to the moral order of the World and to the happiness of man, that arguments which enforce it cannot be drawn from too many sources..."*

John Quincy Adams said, *"So great is my veneration of the Bible, that the earlier my children begin to read it the more confident will be my hope that they will prove useful citizens of their country and respectable members of society."*

Andrew Jackson, hero of the Battle of New Orleans and the War of 1812 and the seventh President, said, *"The Bible is the rock on which our republic rests."*

Benjamin Harrison said, *"If you take out your statutes, your constitution, your family life all that is taken from the Sacred Book, what would there be left to bind society together?"*

Abraham Lincoln, the great emancipator, whom Arthur Schlessinger, Jr. says was the most religious of all the Presidents, said, *"In regard to the great Book, I have only to say that it is the best gift which God has given to man."*

Ulysses S. Grant, commanding general of the Union forces that brought an end to slavery, and elected President after the Civil War, sent a message to *The Sunday School Times.*. He said, *"My advice to Sunday Schools, no matter what their denomination is,*

'Hold fast to the Bible as the sheet anchor of your liberties. Write its precepts in your hearts, and practice them in your lives. To the influence of this Book are we indebted for all the progress made in true civilization, and to this we must look as our guide in the future. 'Righteousness exalteth a nation: but sin is a reproach to any people.'"

William McKinley, 25th President said: *"The more profoundly we study this wonderful book, and the more closely we observe its divine precepts, the better citizens we will become and the higher will be our destiny as a nation."*

Theodore Roosevelt, 26th President, said, *"Almost every man who has by his life-work added to the sum of human achievement of which the race is proud, of which our people are proud, almost every such man has based his life-work largely upon the teachings of the Bible."*

Woodrow Wilson, 28th President, said, *"There are a good many problems before the American people today, and before me as President, but I expect to find the solution of those problems just in the proportion that I am faithful in the study of the Word of God."*

Why such praise for one Book? Because its Author is God, the omnipotent, omniscient, loving, sovereign Creator of man and the universe.

Certainly the Bible claims to be the Word of God. Over and over again the affirmation is made that while the pen used is the pen of man, the words given are the words of God. More than 3,000 times do the writers of Scripture say that what they wrote down, they received from God.

The following Scriptures are but a few instances of its claim to Divine inspiration: *"All scripture is given by inspiration of God, and is profitable for doctrine, for reproof, for correction, for instruction in righteousness."* (II Tim. 3:16)

"For no prophecy ever came by the will of man; but men spake from God, being moved by the Holy Spirit." (I Peter 1:21)

"Then Jeremiah called Baruch the son of Neriah: and Baruch wrote from the mouth of Jeremiah all the words of the Lord, which he had spoken unto him, upon a roll of a book." (Jer. 36:4)

The chapter containing the Ten Commandments begins, *"And God spake all these words, saying..."* (Exodus 20:1)

Not only do the writers claim inspiration from God; Jesus Christ, the Son of God, accepted the Scriptures as being inspired of God, quoting from them many times in His teaching. He referred to Adam and Eve, Jonah and the whale, Moses and his miracles as accepted truth. Even those who disagreed with His teachings, did not disagree with Him on that. That the Scriptures were inspired of God, not one disputed. There were many interpretations, but all believed in the literal inspiration of the Scriptures.

Jesus, as well as the others, considered every word in the original as being inspired, saying, *"Till heaven and earth pass, one jot or one tittle shall in no wise pass from the law, till all be fulfilled."* (Matt. 5:18) Even the smallest letter and mark of the Hebrew Bible was inspired.

Clarence Hall, a war correspondent, wrote the following remarkable news story during World War II: *"Shimmabuke is a tiny village I came upon as a war correspondent in Okinawa. Thirty years before, an American missionary en route to Japan had stopped there just long enough to make two converts—Shosei Kina and his brother, Mojon. He left a Bible with them and passed on. For thirty years they had no contact with any other Christian missionary.*

But they made the Bible come alive. They taught the other villagers until every man, woman, and child in Shimmabuke became a Christian. Shosei Kina became the headman of the village, and Mojon the chief teacher. In the school the Bible was read daily. The precepts of the Bible were law in the village. In those thirty years there developed a Christian democracy in its purest form.

"When the American army came across the island, an advance patrol swept up to the village compound with guns leveled. The two old men stepped forth, bowed low, and began to speak. An interpreter explained that the old men were welcoming the Americans as fellow Christians!

"The flabbergasted GIs sent for their Chaplain. He came with officers of the Intelligence Service. They toured the village. They were astounded at the spotlessly clean homes and streets and the gentility of the inhabitants. The other Okinawan villages they had seen were filthy, and the people were ignorant and poverty-stricken.

"Later I strolled through Shimmabuke with a tough army sergeant. He said, 'I can't figure it out—this kind of people coming from a Bible and a couple of old guys who wanted to be like Jesus Christ. Maybe we have been using the wrong kind of weapons to make the world over!"

CHAPTER 5

COLUMBUS DISCOVERS AMERICA

October 12, 1492 Columbus discovered America. Contrary to the popular belief of the day, Columbus believed that the world was round. He believed that by sailing West, he would eventually reach the East.

Some poke fun at Columbus for thinking he had discovered a new route to the Indies; others consider him a saint, referring to him as St. Columbo. Still others, today, think of him as the very devil, himself, for bringing Western European civilization to the unspoiled continent of the Americas. They insist that Columbus Day should be replaced with "Ethnic Diversity" day. Columbus bashing and Western-civilization bashing has become the *"in"* thing for the *"politically correct."*

But, America in 1492 was no Paradise, no Eden, as some would like to think. Just as in Europe the strong oppressed and enslaved the weak. There was constant warfare between the tribes.

The Aztecs, were a highly *"civilized"* people with a capital (*now Mexico City*), larger than the city of London at that time. They practiced human sacrifice to their *"Corn god"*. The highest offering that could be made to their god was the beating human heart. When the Aztec king, Montezuma II was crowned in 1502, 5,000 were sacrificed and had their hearts ripped from their bodies. When the temple was dedicated to the *"corn god"*, 20,000 were sacrificed.

Surely, it is true, that the coming of the European to America brought tremendous changes, both good and bad. There was cruelty and oppression practiced by each against the other with no room for either, *"...to cast the first stone, being without sin.."* For, *"There is none righteous, no not one:... all have sinned, and come short of the glory of God."* (Rom. 3:10, 23)

With Columbus's voyages, people, animals, plants, diseases, and religious ideas passed between the continents. Europe brought the horse to the Americas; the Americas gave the potato to Europe, a simple vegetable that later saved whole regions from starvation.

Columbus did not sail to America to conquer its people. He was looking for a new trade route to India. To blame Columbus for the cruelties that may have been practiced toward the Indians, is like blaming the inventor of the automobile for all the carnage that has followed through the years on our nation's highways.

Christopher Columbus was named after St. Christopher. The name means literally, *"Christ bearer."* According to legend, St. Christopher was a great hulk of a man who went forth in search of Christ. A holy hermit said, *"Knowest thou that river without a bridge that can only be crossed at peril of drowning?" "I do,"* said Christopher. *"Very well, do thou, who art so tall and strong take up thine abode by the river bank, and assist poor travelers to cross."* So Christopher built him a cabin by the river bank and, with the aid of a tree trunk as staff, carried wayfarers across on his broad shoulders.

One night the big fellow was asleep in his cabin when he heard the voice of a Child cry, *"Christopher! come and set me across."* Out he came, staff in hand; and took the Infant on his shoulders.

But as he waded through the river the Child's weight increased so that it became almost unbearable. He struggled through to the other bank. *"Marvel not, Christopher,"* replied the Child, *"for thou hast borne upon thy back the whole world and Him who created it. I am the Christ whom thou servest in doing good."*

This story would certainly have meant much to the boy,Christopher. He conceived his destiny to carry the divine word of that Holy Child across the mighty ocean to countries steeped in heathen darkness.

Although Columbus spoke of his own ignorance, he knew Latin

and several other languages. In a letter to the Spanish Sovereigns, King Ferninand and Queen Isabella in 1501, he said, *"...today it is forty years that I am navigating through all those parts of the world which are navigated today. ...In the carrying out of this enterprise of the Indies, neither reason nor mathematics nor maps were any use to me: fully accomplished were the words of Isaiah."*

Columbus was a student of the Bible, and Isaiah says, *"It is He (God) that sitteth upon the circle (sphere) of the earth..."* (Isaiah 40:22) In a time when the most up to date scientific opinion was that the earth rested on the backs of two huge Elephants, standing on the back of a huge Turtle swimming in a great sea, the Bible said, *"He (God)...hangeth the earth upon nothing.* (Job 26:7)

The first thing that Columbus did when he landed in the New World was to plant a cross. In 1892, in commemoration of the 400th anniversary of the landing of Columbus, the U. S. Post Office issued a two-cent stamp showing Columbus planting that cross.

After convincing Queen Isabella of the rightness of his beliefs, he set sail with three small ships, the Pinta, the Nina, and the Santa Maria. He had a total complement of 120 men, 90 being crew and 30 officers and observers. The Santa Maria, the flagship, of 233 tons, was the largest.

After 21 days elapsed, without sight of land, the courage of the crew began to sink. Columbus' faith was severely tested, as the crew threatened mutiny. Finally, however, signs of land were seen, including large numbers of birds. Columbus sailed in the direction from which the birds flew, and promised a reward to the first man to sight land. A cannon shot announced the discovery of land at two o'clock in the morning.

Soon many natives gathered on the beach. Columbus later describes them as having coarse black hair with handsome bodies and good faces painted with black, red or white paint. He wrote, *"I recognized that they were people who would be better..converted to our Holy Faith by love than by force. To some of them I gave red caps, and glass beads which they put on their chests, and many other things of small value, in which they took so much pleasure and became so much our friends that it was a marvel."*

Thinking he had sailed around the world to the Indies, off the coast of eastern Asia, he called the new land, Indies, and the natives, Indians. When he returned to Spain with the news of his discovery, he was greeted with acclamations, the thunder of cannon, and ringing of bells. On Palm Sunday, as he entered Seville, he was a sensation as he introduced the *"Indians"* he brought back, along with gold ornaments, pearls, parrots, and other tokens of the new lands. He was received by the king and queen at Barcelona and unprecedented honors were accorded him. The sovereigns actually rose to greet him and a seat was placed for him near the throne.

What a beautiful picture of the Christian being received by the King of Kings and Lord of Lords, Jesus Christ. One of these days, after sailing through the uncharted seas of life with our faith tested at every turn, we will arrive at our heavenly home.

We have not discovered a new land, but a new life, through faith in Jesus Christ. If there is *"joy in heaven over one sinner that repenteteth"* (Luke 5:7), surely there will be even greater rejoicing when we enter heaven's gates and the throne room of heaven. When Stephen, the first martyr, was being stoned to death for faithfully preaching the gospel of Christ, he saw *"the heavens opened and the Son of Man standing on the right hand of God"* (Acts 8:56)

In Hebrews we are told that Jesus *"...after He had offered one sacrifice for sins, forever, (His own death on the cross) sat down on the right hand of God"* (Heb. 10:12). Even as King Ferdinand and Queen Isabella stood up to receive Columbus, so Jesus stood up to receive his faithful servant, Stephen.

CHAPTER 6

POCAHONTAS FINDS TRUE LOVE IN JAMESTOWN

The landing at Jamestown began as a dream planted in the heart of Richard Hakluyt, an Anglican clergyman and one of England's great Renaissance geographers during the last half of the sixteenth century. It was Hakluyt's lifelong passion to see the North American continent explored, settled, and evangelized for Christ. He *envisioned* villages, towns, and cities in America where Indians and settlers could live in peace and prosperity.

He had read the letters of the Spanish explorer, Cortez, with their frightening tales from the New World of human sacrifices by the Aztecs to gods of wood and stone. He read heartbreaking accounts of the misery of these people who lived in bondage to pagan practices, constant tribal rivalry and warfare. He sincerely believed that the love of Christ for the whole world *compelled* him to take that love to the Indians.

Finally, in 1606, Richard Hakluyt's efforts to establish a permanent settlement in Virginia resulted in the Virginia Charter from King James I. It was the same King James that authorized the English translation of the "King James Bible", published in 1611. The charter reads: "*We would vouchsafe unto them our Licence, to make Habitation, Plantation, and to deduce a colony of sundry of our people into that Part of America commonly called Virginia...by the Providence of Almighty God,... propagating of Christian religion to such People, as yet live in Darkness ...*"

On Dec. 20, 1606, an expedition, commanded by Captain Christopher Newport, sailed from London. After a stormy crossing, they finally sighted land, April 26, 1607. A small scouting party of militia headed by Captain John Smith was sent out to explore the lay of the land. Finally, on April 29, as the others were disembarking, John Smith, his soldiers, and the ship's carpenter erected a large wooden cross on the beach at Cape Henry. They had carried it all the way from England for this very time. On that first day, they knelt at the foot of that cross, as they were led in a prayer of thanksgiving by their Chaplain, Robert Hunt. It was the *first* public prayer of the *first* permanent settlement in America.

After landing at Cape Henry, sailing up the James River, and establishing their rough log fortress at Jamestown, the settlers faced a new round of trials: bad weather, short supplies, unfriendly Indians, inadequate and rotting foodstuffs. In one settler's words, "*Scarse ten amongst us coulde either goe or well stand; such extreame weaknes and sicknes oppressed us.*"

Captain Newport sailed back to England for help, leaving 104 men to build that first permanent settlement on America's soil. By September 10, half the settlers were dead. In January 1608, the wooden church and many of the log homes of the settlers burned, including the home of Chaplain Hunt.

Captain John Smith, reporting later, wrote, "*Good Master Hunt, our preacher, lost all his library, and all that he had (but the clothes on his back) yet none ever saw him repine at his loss.*" (Being a "*Bookaholic*" myself, I know how he must have felt.) Smith went on to say, "*We had daily Common Prayer morning and evening, every Sunday two sermons, and every three months the holy Communion, till our minister died.*" Of Hunt's life among them, he concluded, "*Till he could not speak, he never ceased to his utmost to animate us constantly to persist.*"

Captain Newport made several trips back to England for supplies. On his second trip, he brought back 70 new settlers. Among them were two women, Mistress Forrest and her maid. A few months later, Ann Burras, the maid, was married to the carpenter, John Laydon. It was the first recorded English marriage on American soil. Their child, *"Virginia"*, born the next year, was the first to be born at Jamestown.

In 1609, 300 men, women and children set sail on the sailing vessel, "Sea Venture". During a horrific storm, it was wrecked on the island of Bermuda, called *"The Isle of Devils"*. One of the passengers was *John Rolfe*, who later married *Pocahontas*.

Rolfe's first daughter by his first wife was born on the island and was named, *"Bermuda"*. After nine months on the island of Bermuda the colonists managed to construct two small boats, the *Patience* and the *Deliverance*, in which they sailed on to Jamestown. Fourteen days later they landed at Jamestown, May 24, 1610.

It was not a pleasant sight that greeted them at Jamestown. Ruin and desolation were everywhere. The winter of 1609-10 in Jamestown has been described through the years as the *"starving time."* It saw the population shrink from 500 to about sixty as a result of disease, sickness, Indian arrows, and malnutrition. It destroyed morale and reduced them to scavengers stalking the forest, fields, and woods for anything that might be used as food.

In the early Spring of 1610, the few weary settlers still alive, decided to give up their dream of a permanent settlement in America and started to sail back to England. *But, God intervened.*

Just a few miles down the river, they met the supply ship of the new governor, Lord De la Warr *(later spelled Delaware)*. They knew that God had answered their prayers, and with their hopes buoyed, decided to return to the colony after all, knowing that God was with them. It was recorded that they had been saved by an act of *"Providence."*

The Jamestown settlers had come to the new world, not only with hopes of it being a profitable venture, but entrusted with the task of taking the gospel of Christ to the Native American Indians.

One of the first, if not the first, to be converted to Christ was an Indian Princess, *Pocahontas,* daughter of *Powhatan,* chief of the *Chickahominy tribe.* It was John Rolfe, who first shared the good news of Christ's love for her, with Pocahontas.

Captain John Smith, during one of his explorations, before

returning to England, was taken prisoner by Powhatan. He was kept as a prisoner for six weeks, expecting to die, but then, he was released and sent back to Jamestown. In 1616, in a letter to the Queen, Smith writes about how he was saved from death by the Indian Princess, *Pocahontas,* daughter of Powhatan. He says that *"at the minute of my execution, she hazarded the beating out of her own brains to save mine."*

Pocahontas often visited the near-starving English settlers, bringing them food from time to time, and warning them of proposed Indian attacks. She accepted Christ as her Savior while in her teens, and was instructed in the Christian faith, and baptized by Rev. Alexander Whitaker. *Pocahontas* chose as her Christian name to be called *"Rebecca"*.

Pocahontas fell in love with John Rolfe. His first wife had died. In 1614 he requested permission to marry her. Her father, Powhatan agreed, and they were married, April 5, 1614, in the Anglican church at Jamestown. The marriage was solemnized in the presence of both Native Americans and English settlers, including her uncle and two brothers. As a result peace reigned between the Indians and the Jamestown settlers, allowing them to establish roots in a new land.

In 1615 the Rolfes' only child, *Thomas,* was born. The next year the family, with several Indian attendants, sailed to England for a visit. The English were delighted with Pocahontas. She was received as royalty. They called her *"Lady Rebecca"*. The Queen received her at the palace, and the Bishop of London entertained her.

In 1617 the Rolfes prepared to return to Virginia, but before they sailed, *Pocahontas* contracted smallpox. She died in March 1617 in Gravesend, England, and is buried at St. George's Church.

Pocahontas is now spending eternity with her *"Heavenly Bridegroom"*, (the Lord, Jesus Christ), whose love for her, she discovered in Jamestown..

CHAPTER 7

PILGRIMS SHARE THANKSGIVING WITH INDIANS

As the "hippie" couple strolled down the street, one said to the other, *"I'm going over and pick up my unemployment check. Then I'll drop in at the university to see what's holding up my check for my federal education grant. After that I'll pick up our food stamps. Meanwhile, you go over to the free clinic and check your tests, and pick up my new glasses at the health center. Then go to the Welfare Department and apply for an increase in our eligibility limit."*

"Then, I'll meet you at 5 o'clock at the Federal Building for the mass demonstration against the rotten Establishment."

How different the attitude of America's first settlers. One-hundred-two Pilgrims, after finally securing sponsorship from some London merchants and frustrating efforts to find sufficient provisions for the voyage, set sail from Plymouth, England, on the Mayflower. Their destination was Virginia. Their pastor, John Robinson, told them as they were about to board, *"I charge you before God that you follow me no further than you have seen me follow the Lord Jesus Christ...for I am verily persuaded that the Lord hath more truth yet to break out of His Holy Word."*

In writing of their departure, some years later, William Bradford said, *"So they left the goodly and pleasant city which had been their resting place...but they knew they were pilgrims and looked not much on those things but lifted their eyes to heaven, their dearest country, and quieted their spirits."*

The 67 day crossing was extremely arduous. The voyagers were crowded below decks amid the stench and darkness of a leaky, wooden vessel. Seasickness was rampant. They had little more to eat than hardtack, dried fish, cheese, and salt beef. Storms were so fierce that they threatened to pound the ship into oblivion. Yet, of the 102, only one young man, William Butten, succumbed to the rigors of the voyage. One baby, Oceanus Hopkins, was born aboard ship.

Instead of reaching their proposed destination, Virginia, storms brought them to anchor off the wild, uncharted coast of New England. William Bradford recounts, *"Being thus passed the vast ocean, they had now no friends to welcome them, no inns to entertain or refresh their weather-beaten bodies, no houses or much less towns to repair to, to seek for succour...And for the season it was winter, and they that know the winters of that country know them to be sharp and violent and subject to cruel and fierce storms. Besides, what could they see but a hideous and desolate wilderness full of wild beasts and wild men."*

Tension fills the air as the men gather in the cramped and gloomy Great Cabin of the Mayflower on Nov. 11, 1620. One by one, the passengers sign the Mayflower Compact which is the first document of self-rule by Europeans in the New World. *"In the name of God...we having undertaken for the glory of God, and advancement of the Christian faith...a voyage to plant the first colony...do by these presents solemnly and mutually in the presence of God...combine ourselves together into a civil Body Politick, for our better Ordering and Preservation, and Furtherance of the Ends aforesaid..."*

On Monday, Dec 11, 1620, after worship services on Sunday, the weary Pilgrims stepped ashore at Plymouth Rock. The winter of 1620-21 blew wet and cold and miserable. Crew and passengers, weakened by crowding, exposure, and improper diet, sickened and died in alarming numbers—six in December, eight in January, seventeen in February. Of March, Bradford wrote: *"This month thirteen of our number died...scarce fifty remain, the living scarce able to bury the dead."* Entire families perished. Of the eighteen married women who landed at Plymouth, only three survived. Baby Oceanus died. To keep Indians from learning of the colony's plight, survivors placed the dead in concealed graves under cover of dark.

Misfortune continued to dog the struggling colony. Mary Allerton gave birth to a son—stillborn. She, too, died several weeks later. Chimney sparks twice ignited the thatched roof of the Common House sheltering the sick—and the colony's store of gunpowder. The fear of Indian attack caused concern, and wolves and wildcats bedeviled the settlers. In February an unseasonable rain accompanied by "the greatest gusts of wind that ever we had" melted the mud-daubed walls of their dwellings. By November 1621, less than half of those that had set foot on Plymouth Rock were still alive.

Through it all, their faith remained strong as they continued to look toward heaven. They would meet their loved ones again. This world was not their home and they were only pilgrims and strangers down here. They were worshiping God in freedom and did not the Bible say, *"All things work together for good to them that love God and are the called according to His purpose."* (Rom. 8:28)

One week after the settlers started their gardens, an Indian strode into the encampment and announced, *"Welcome."* Autumn brought a plenteous harvest. In late November, *"the governor sent four men on fowling, that so we might after a special manner rejoice together."* A single day's shooting yielded the hunters *"as much fowl as.... served the company almost a week."* The Indian chief, Massasoit, arrived with some 90 tribesmen; contributed five deer, and for three days red man and white celebrated with thanksgiving to God.

America's first Thanksgiving Proclamation was made by Governor Bradford in which he stated, *"Inasmuch as the great Father has given us this year an abundant harvest of Indian corn, wheat, peas, beans, squashes, and garden vegetables, and has made the forests to abound with game and the sea with fish and clams, and inasmuch as*

He has protected us from the ravages of the savages...has granted us freedom to worship God according to the dictates of our own conscience.

"Now I, your magistrate, do proclaim that all ye Pilgrims, with your wives and ye little ones, do gather at ye meeting house, on ye hill, between the hours of 9 and 12 in the day time, on Thursday, November 29th...there to listen to ye pastor and render thanksgiving to ye Almighty God for all His blessings."

Missionary Benjamin Weir was held hostage in Lebanon and imprisoned under miserable conditions for 16 months. In his first interview after his release, he was asked how he spent his time and how he dealt with boredom and despair. His answer stunned the reporters. He simply said, "Counting my blessings."

"Blessings?" they responded.

"Yes," he explained. "Some days I got to take a shower. Sometimes there were some vegetables in my food. And I could always be thankful for the love of my family."

Paul and Silas, though they were beaten, thrown into prison, and placed in stocks, were still "singing hymns to God". (Acts 16:25).

"In everything give thanks." (1 Thess. 5:18)

CHAPTER 8

A DECLARATION OF DEPENDENCE

The day is July 4, 1776. The place is Philadelphia. The occasion is the meeting of the Continental Congress. The purpose is the approval of a document written by a 33 year old Virginia farmer and lawyer, Thomas Jefferson. The oldest man there is Benjamin Franklin who is 70. There are 56 men, (lawyers, doctors, farmers, soldiers, merchants, manufacturers, educators); all gathered to sign one of the most important documents the world has ever seen, the Declaration of Independence.

This Declaration of Independence declared, freedom and equality for all men. It was the beginning of a new experiment in the governments of men. And because of this document, today, America stands as the champion of all freedom loving peoples of the world. As a result of the Declaration of Independence, to be born in America is one of the greatest blessings that can befall any person on this earth.

In the Declaration of Independence our forefathers wrote: "*We hold these truths to be self-evident that all men are created equal, that they are endowed by their CREATOR with certain inalienable rights... We, therefore, the Representatives of the United States of America in General Congress assembled, appealing to the SUPREME JUDGE of the world... And for the support of this declaration, with a firm reliance on the protection of DIVINE PROVIDENCE we mutually pledge to each other our lives, our fortunes, and our sacred honor.*"

The Declaration of Independence was not only a *declaration of independence* but a *declaration of dependence*. Dependence on God.

George Washington said, "*It is impossible rightly to govern the world without God and the Bible.*" Benjamin Franklin said, "*God governs in the affairs of men... We have been assured in the Sacred Writings that 'Except the Lord build the house, they labour in vain that build it.' I firmly believe this, and I also believe that without His concurring aid we shall proceed in this political building no better than the builders of Babel.*" Perhaps, with the *Babel* of confusion that reigns in our land today, it is time we returned to the faith of America's founding fathers.

John Adams wrote, "*Independence Day ought to be commemorated as the day of deliverance by solemn acts of devotion to God Almighty.*" Inscribed on the Liberty Bell that pealed out the news of the Declaration is a quotation from the Bible, "*Proclaim liberty throughout all the land unto all the inhabitants thereof.*" (Lev. 25:10)

Sometimes we forget that the British Empire with its vast army and far flung navy was, at that time, the most powerful force in the world. The signers of the Declaration of Independence *knew* that *without* God's help, the rag tag, ill-equipped, undisciplined militia of the colonies in America would be massacred. Yet, they chose to risk the hangman's noose for freedom. John Hancock wrote large, he said, when he signed his name to the Declaration of Independence, so that King George would have no trouble reading it.

John Hancock was president of the Continental Congress and presided over the framing of the Declaration of Independence. One day he went to hear another signer of the Declaration, a Presbyterian clergyman, John Witherspoon. Witherspoon was not only a pastor, but president of Princeton University. The text of his sermon that day was, "*I (Jesus) am the door; by me if any man enter in, he shall be saved... I am come that they might have life, and that they might have it more abundantly.*" (Jn 10:9,10)

Although Hancock had attended church all his life and was a graduate of Harvard, he couldn't comprehend how Jesus could be a *"door"*. He mulled it over as he made his way home. Then, as he put the key in the lock, opened the door and stepped out of the darkness outside into the lighted room where his family was waiting, he shouted, *"Now, I see!!"* His wife said, *"Of course you see, it was dark outside and you came into the light.* Hancock replied, *"No—now I see—Jesus is the door and faith is the key that unlocks the door. I accepted Him as my personal Saviour when I came through the door and I am saved."*

The Fifty-six courageous men who signed the Declaration of Independence *understood* that this was not *just* high-sounding rhetoric. They knew that if they succeeded, the best they could expect would be years of hardship in a struggling new nation. If they lost, they would be put to death as traitors.

Of the fifty-six, few were long to survive. Five were captured by the British and tortured before they died. Twelve had their homes sacked, looted, occupied by the enemy, or burned. Two lost their sons in the army. One had two sons captured. Nine of the fifty-six died in the war, from its hardships or from its bullets.

It is important to remember that these men were not poor men, or wild-eyed pirates. They were men of means; rich men, most of them, who enjoyed much ease and luxury in their personal lives. *Not* hungry men, desperate men with nothing to lose, but prosperous men, wealthy landowners, secure in their prosperity, and respected in their communities.

But they *considered* liberty much more important than the security they enjoyed, and they pledged their lives, their fortunes, and their sacred honor. They paid the price. Freedom was won. Someone has said, *"To be born free is a privilege. To die free is an awesome responsibility."*

Picture King George III the day he received this traitorous document from the colonies. He must have been furious. He was king, after all, and the king made the laws, *not* the people. Now his lowly subjects in America were declaring their independence and refusing to obey his laws. They were appealing to a higher law—the "Laws of Nature and of Natures's God."

These words had very specific meaning in the eighteenth century. Sir William Blackstone, the great teacher of the English common law, upon which America's laws are based, wrote: *"Man, con-*

sidered as a creature, must necessarily be subject to the laws of his Creator, for he is entirely a dependent being... And, consequently, as man depends absolutely upon his Maker for everything, it is necessary that he should in all points conform to his Maker's will. This will of his Maker, is called the law of nature... Upon these two foundations, the law of Nature and the law of Revelation (the Bible), depend all human law; that is to say, no human laws should be suffered to contradict these."

From childhood, the men who wrote and signed the Declaration of Independence heard these truths from the Bible. They were read to them by their parents; they were taught to them in their schools and universities; and they were preached to them in their churches on Sunday morning.

The signers of America's most treasured document, believed that every man, woman, and child (*born and unborn*) was created by God, and that God, their Creator, loved each of them equally.

"For God so loved the world (every human being) that He gave His only begotten Son that whosoever (anyone) believeth on Him (Jesus Christ) shall not perish but have everlasting life" (John 3:16)

They believed the words of the apostle Peter when he said, "*Of a truth I perceive that God is no respecter of persons: But in every nation he that feareth Him, and worketh righteousness, is accepted with Him.*" (Acts 10:34,35)

It is, *ONLY*, as we *DECLARE* our DEPENDENCE upon GOD, that we can be *truly* happy and *truly* free.

On July 8, 1776, the *"Liberty Bell"* was rung for the proclamation of the Declaration of Independence. On Oct. 4, 1781, the bell rang out for the surrender of Cornwallis. July 4, 1826, it tolled the death of Thomas Jefferson and John Adams, who both died on the same day, exactly 50 years after the Declaration of Independence was signed.

CHAPTER 9

AMERICA'S MIRACLE REVOLUTION

For over 200 years millions of patriotic Americans have answered the call of their country to leave the comfort of their homes and family to lay their lives on the line to fight that America might become free and remain free. Thousands have sacrificed with their very lives, not only for America's freedom but the freedom of others.

The freedoms we enjoy as spelled out in the Declaration of Independence and the Constitution were won at terrible cost and sacrifice on the part of America's first veterans.

In the 1700's the British Empire was the greatest power on earth, and yet a few thousand ill-clothed, ill-fed, ill-equipped patriots under the dedicated and prayerful leadership of General George Washington wrested themselves free from tyranny.

When Patrick Henry echoed forth, *"Give me liberty or give me death"*, he was but expressing the deepest feelings of all. *It is not those who have actually suffered under the heavy iron fist of totalitarianism that wimpishly mutter, "Better Red than dead".*

Freedom is so dear to the spirit of man that no sacrifice is considered too great. This is why, that, as Nathan Hale was being hanged by the British, he defiantly proclaimed, *"My only regret is that I have but one life to give for my country."*

At Woodstock, Virginia, on January 28, 1776 Lutheran Pastor, Peter Muhlenberg, close friend of both George Washington and Patrick Henry, preached on the text: *"There is a time to every purpose under heaven...a time for war, and a time of peace."* (Eccl. 3:1-8)

At the close of the sermon he dramatically threw aside his clerical robe and revealed that he was wearing the uniform of a Colonel in the Continental Army. He declared that the time to fight had come and recruited from his Parish and others a Regiment of men to do battle. It was the Eighth Virginia Regiment, famous as the "*German Regiment*" which served with such conspicuous honor during the Revolution.

The winter of 1777 was an especially harsh one. The troops at Valley Forge were virtually shelterless; they suffered horribly and "*remained whole days without provisions.*" But the Prussian Baron von Steuben, determined to train the men in a system of military formations and drill, kept them profitably occupied for the duration. An almost certain defeat was turned into a victory. The army emerged from the "*winter of discontent*", a far more potent striking force.

In a major address before the Assembly of Connecticut in 1783, Ezra Stiles, then president of Yale, reviewed the events of the American Revolution and suggested why near disasters time and again suddenly turned to victories.

"In our lowest and most dangerous state, in 1776 and 1777, we sustained ourselves against the British army of sixty thousand troops, commanded by...the ablest generals Britain could procure throughout Europe, with a naval force of twenty-two thousand seaman in above eighty British men-of-war."

"*Who, but a Washington, inspired by Heaven,*" asked Stiles, "*could have conceived the surprise move upon the enemy at Princeton—that Christmas eve, when Washington and his army crossed the Delaware?*

"*Who but the Ruler of the winds,*" he asked, "*could have delayed British reinforcements by three months of contrary ocean winds at a critical point of the war?*

"*Or what but a providential miracle,*" he insisted, "*at the last minute detected the treacherous scheme of traitor Benedict Arnold, which would have delivered the American army, including George Washington himself, into the hands of the enemy?"*

One of the most famous battles of the Revolution was the battle of *"King's Mountain"* in South Carolina, considered by historians as a major turning point of the war. Things were not going well in the North at the time, for the armies of General Washington. Discouragement and fear of ultimate defeat was at a peak.

By the late summer of 1780, British forces controlled Georgia, South Carolina, and New York City. Lord Cornwallis devised a plan to quickly end the *"rebellion of the colonies,"* by landing an army of British in the South, driving through North Carolina, and linking up with a British army in Virginia. No Patriot force of any consequence opposed him, except the scattered *"backwoods men"* on both sides of the Blue Ridge mountains in Virginia, North Carolina, and what became Tennessee.

To quell their resistance, Cornwallis dispatched a thousand men under Colonel Patrick Ferguson. In response, a few hundred stubborn frontier riflemen rallied, marched through the snow across the rugged Blue Ridge plateau and on King's Mountain, October 7, 1780, decimated Ferguson's command.

Continental forces in the North, hearing the news of this miraculous victory over the greatly superior force of the British by a few *"ignorant"* but *"inspired"* backwoodsmen, encouraged them to fight on. In a year and a week later, Cornwallis surrendered to Washington at Yorktown.

"But now for the rest of the story," as Paul Harvey might say. The story behind the story. Circuit riding preacher, Samuel Doak, Presbyterian, standing on a tree stump as his pulpit under some nearby shade trees at Sycamore Shoals, in the wilderness of Tennessee, preached a sermon that changed history on September 26, 1780. He was a graduate of both Washington and Lee, and Princeton Universities. After the Revolution he founded two colleges and at age 65 took up the study of Chemistry and Hebrew.

Several hundred backwoodsmen had gathered there with their rifles to try somehow to stop the march of the British in the South to what seemed certain victory. As the mountain men in their hunting shirts stood bareheaded with caps in hand under the warm September sun, Rev. Doak lifted his eyes to the blue barrier of the mountains, above which the sun had just risen, and recounted the saga of Gideon and the Lord's 300 in the 7th chapter of Judges.

He told how by God's direction and power, Gideon and just 300 wholly dedicated men defeated the thousands of the Midianites. He told how when they shouted, *"The sword of the Lord and of Gideon"*, the armies of the Midianites were put to flight and defeated.

The preacher held wide his arms and shouted, *"Let that be your battle cry: The sword of the Lord and of Gideon"*. Like slow thunder the shout rolled back from that patriotic band gathered that day, "The sword of the Lord and Gideon."

They knelt to pray for God's help and strength. When the last "*Amen*" was said, they mounted their horses and turned up Gap Creek toward the blue mountains. The *"preacher"* also mounted his horse and with rifle in hand moved out with them to fight for freedom.

At their first place of encampment on the way to King's Mountain and their place in history, there is today a bronze plaque which reads:

FIRST NIGHT ENCAMPMENT OF
KING'S MOUNTAIN MEN,
SEPTEMBER 26, 1780
"THEY TRUSTED IN GOD
AND KEPT THEIR POWDER DRY"

CHAPTER 10

THE *"STAR SPANGLED BANNER"* STILL WAVES

It is a symbol of our country and what it stands for. It has inspired great feats of valour and bravery. During World War II, when U. S. Marines captured Iwo Jima, its planting as a symbol of victory was recorded for posterity by an Associated Press photographer and widely publicized, inspiring others to fight on.

It is a symbol of one's love and devotion to country as it is drapped over the casket of those who have valiantly and sacrificially served their country even unto death. It was a symbol of a lack of devotion to country, (*as aid and comfort was given to the enemy*), when angry protestors shamefully spit upon, trampled upon and burned it, during the Vietnam War.

It stands as a symbol of unparalleled bravery and American scientific knowhow, when it was planted triumphantly by astronauts on the moon. It is the flag of the United States of America.

It was June 14, 1777. Congress, recognizing the necessity for a national flag, passed a resolution specifying: *"That the flag of the thirteen United States be thirteen stripes, alternate red and white, that the union be thirteen stars, white in a blue field representing a new constellation."*

General George Washington, Colonel George Ross and Robert Morris had been commissioned by Congress to develop the design. Tradition says that they paid a visit to a young Philadelphia widow, Betsy Ross, who supported herself and children by her excellent needle work. George Ross was her deceased husband's uncle.

They described the design for the flag they had in mind and she agreed to do the job. She recommended, however, that five-pointed rather than six-pointed stars be used and it was agreed.

General Washington, whose coat of arms had red and white stripes with white stripes on a blue field, once expressed his theory on the symbolism of the *"Stars and Stripes"*. He said, *"We took the star from Heaven, the red from our mother country, separating it by white stripes, thus showing that we have separated from her, and the white stripes shall go down to posterity representing liberty."*

A number of flags with different design, other than the one officially adopted by Congress on that day, were flown during the Revolution to inspire the troops. One had a *"ready rifleman"* on a red background and the words of Patrick Henry, *"Liberty or Death."* Another had a *"coiled rattlesnake"* and the words, *"Don't Tread on Me."*

Another flag was one that was flown above Fort Moultrie in Charleston Harbor during one of the most famous battles of the Revolution. It was June 28, 1776. Early in the attack, the flag fell outside the parapet. Sergeant William Jasper leaped after it under a rain of bullets, crying, *"Don't let us fight without a flag."* He replaced it amid the cheers of his fellow patriots. After a ten-hour attack, the British forces withdrew. This flag that inspired such bravery contained a crescent and the word, *"Liberty"*, on a blue field.

It is believed that the first time *"Old Glory"* or the *"Stars and Stripes"* was flown in battle was over Fort Schuyler, Rome, New York, August 3, 1777. The garrison of brave soldiers was under seige by the British, and supplies were almost exhausted. But they were determined to hold the fort. Hearing about the new flag recently adopted by Congress, the officers hastily constructed a flag out of a red petticoat, a white ammunition shirt, and a blue cloak, belonging to Captain Abraham Swarthout. Proudly it was unfurled above the fort in defiance of their attackers, giving the men of America's fledgling army courage to hang on.

During the War of 1812, a young Washington lawyer, Francis Scott Key, found himself held captive aboard a British ship outside the city of Baltimore, near Fort McHenry. All through the night, through the mist and drizzle, he watched *"the rockets' red glare, the bombs bursting in air"*, as the British navy bombarded Baltimore and Fort McHenry. They had already taken Washington and burned its government buildings to the ground.

At day break as the mists cleared away, he could see the American flag still flying above the fort. Intensely moved, he composed the *"Star Spangled Banner"*, scribbling the first draft on the back of an envelope. The flag that flew over Fort McHenry that night and so inspired the writing of our national anthem is preserved today in the National Museum in Washington, D.C.

Although seldom sung, the last stanza of this anthem that brings us to our feet in patriotic fervor, expresses the faith of its author. *"O thus be it ever when freemen shall stand, Between their lov'd home & the war's desolation! Blest with vict'ry & peace may the heav'n rescued land, Praise the power that hath made & preserv'd us a nation! Then conquer we must, when our cause it is just, And this be our motto 'In God is our Trust: And the star spangled banner in triumph shall wave O'er the land of the free & the home of the brave."*

Francis Scott Key was a prime mover in the founding of the American Sunday School Union. The ASSU has been instrumental in the establishing of thousands of Sunday Schools throughout America, especially in rural, pioneer areas.

The pledge of allegiance to the flag was first composed by Francis Bellamy in 1892, *(400th anniversary of the discovery of America)* to celebrate Columbus Day in the public schools, and then on Flag Day, June 14, 1954, Congress passed and President Dwight Eisenhower signed into law a bill which added to the pledge the phrase, *"UNDER GOD".*

Senator John McCain of Arizona was a prisoner of the communists in North Vietnam for more than five years during the

Vietnam war. He tells of how one of his buddies, a fellow POW, made a needle of bamboo, and with thread and pieces from his ragged pajama like clothing, sewed an American flag on the inside of his shirt. Every morning he and his fellow prisoners would stand at attention and with the inside of his shirt exposed, proudly pledge their allegiance to the flag of the United States of America.

One day the communist guards found out about it; dragged him out of his cell and beat him until his face was so mishapen that he was unrecognizable. They ripped out the flag on the inside of his shirt and threw him back into the cell.

McCain said he looked over at his buddy the next morning. There he sat, face swollen, body aching, with another bamboo needle, sewing another American flag.

"It was," says Senator McCain, *"our daily pledges of allegiance to the flag of the country we loved, that kept us alive through those terrible years."*

How thankful we are that because of such patriots as this, we can still be reminded that there is a God and we are a nation under God as we reverently *"Pledge allegiance to the flag of the United States of America and to the republic for which it stands: one nation UNDER GOD, indivisible, with liberty and justice for all."*

CHAPTER 11

REVOLUTIONS THAT FAILED

It was July 14, 1789. An angry mob had gathered outside the gates of the Bastille in Paris. The notorious prison was heavily fortified and guarded by the king's army. It had stood for four centuries, but it was no match for the fearsome wrath felt by the populace as they stormed it that day. It was leveled to the ground.

Inspired by the American Revolution and desirous of the freedoms it won, the French in 1789 revolted against the monarchy of Louis XVI. Thousands were herded (men, women, and children) to the guillotine, often for no greater crime than that they were of royal birth. Many others were massacred by roving bands of the Revolutionary Army. Churches were closed and converted into temples of *"reason"*.

While the French desired to achieve the same sort of freedom that the Americans enjoyed they tried to do it by an atheistic, rationalistic, humanistic, secular approach that was far different from the basis of American democracy. The Russian Communist Revolution was patterned after the French. Both failed.

Under the French system the individual renounced his natural, God-given rights and liberties for the sake of the will of the State. The rights of the minority had no Protection. There was no concept of responsibility to a Supreme Being to whom all men must answer for their deeds. The writings and theories of the atheist philosophers, Voltaire, Robespierre and others were substituted for the Bible.

As a result, the democratic experiment of the Republic of France lasted only a few years In 1804 Napoleon Bonaparte was crowned Emperor of France and established a dictatorship as bad or worse than the Monarchy of Louis XVI.

Concerning the French Revolution, the French political philosopher, Alexis de Tocqueville, wrote: *"Passionate and persistent efforts were made to wean men away from the faith of their fathers...Irreligion became an all-prevailing passion, fierce, intolerant and predatory."*

Voltaire wrote: *"We cannot destroy Christianity until we first destroy the Christian Sabbath".* So it was decreed that one day in ten be a day of rest instead of one in seven. It was disastrous. Even the horses, going for 10 days without rest, broke down in the streets under the strain.

With the typical arrogance and condescension of the atheist toward those who believe in God, Voltaire commented on something the great physicist, Sir Isaac Newton, had written.

Newton, who was a devout Christian and ardent Bible student wrote concerning the prophecy in Daniel 12:4, *"...many shall run to and fro, and knowledge shall be increased"* that man would one day be able to travel at the fantasttc speed of 50 miles per hour. Voltaire commented: *"The poor dotard! Everyone knows that at that speed, a man wouldn't be able to breath and he would die."*

Although the fumes of atheism constantly spewed from his mouth and pen, Voltaire at times had doubts about his atheism. He once said: *"The world embarrasses me, and I cannot think that this watch exists and has no Watchmaker."*

Voltaire was a very unhappy man. Before his death, he said, *"I wish I had never been born."* Robespierre tried to commit suicide but failed. With poetic justice, he lost his head on the same guillotine that thousands of innocents had lost theirs because of him.

How different was the American Revolution. Professor Louis Hartz of Yale wrote in the *"American Political Science Review"* that the revolutionary thinkers of America were not like the secular prophets, Robespierre and Voltaire. He says, *"...the Americans refused to join in the Great Enlightenment enterprise of shattering the*

Christian concept of sin, replacing it with an unlimited humanism, and then emerging with an earthly paradise as glittering as the heavenly one that had been destroyed."

Lenin (1870-1924) studied law at Kazan and Petrograd (*Leningrad*), where he became familiar with the works of Karl Marx and the evolutionary theories of Darwin. In 1900 he went to Switzerland where he organized an underground party to lead the working classes of Russia in overthrowing the Russian government. In 1903 Lenin and the Bolsheviks led the Social Democratic party to promote the *"dictatorship of the proletariat,"* which eventually resulted in the overthrow of the Czar in 1917.

The Social Democratic party became the Communist party, and by promising to divide up the landed estates in Russia among the peasants, won their support. It wasn't long, however, until everything became the property of the State, including the individual. Lenin promised that a classless *"worker's paradise"* would evolve when the evolutionary theories of Marx's *"dialectical materialism"* (*without God*) took over the world.

Lenin wrote: *"Marxism is materialism. As such it is without mercy for religion. Every religious idea of God, even flirting with the idea of God, is unutterable vileness."*

He also wrote, even before he came to power, that the French Revolution did not last because they had not killed enough people. He said, *"It is necessary to learn the art of accepting political compromises, schemes, zig-zags, maneuvers of conciliation and retreat, in short all the maneuvers necessary to accelerate the taking over of political power...It is necessary...to practice everything possible; tricks, guiles, illegal methods: ready to suppress and conceal what is the truth: in short, it is in the interest of the struggle of the classes that we reduce our morals."*

Concerning the church, he said, *"We must wage a merciless battle against the reactionary clergy and suppress its resistance with such cruelty that it will remember...The more members of the reactionary bourgeoisie we manage to shoot, the better. It is precisely now that we must* give such a lesson to these characters that they would not dare to think of any resistance."

In 1903 Lenin had exactly 17 followers. Fourteen years later, in 1917, he overthrew the mighty Russian empire with only 40,000 Party members. In 70 years the Communist Party controlled the lives of billions.

Krushchev once boasted, *"Whether you like it or not, history is on our side. We will bury you. I can prophesy that your grandchildren in America will live under socialism."*

Magnificent statues were erected to the glory of the Communist *"god"*, Lenin. When Lenin died, his body was embalmed and put on display in the Kremlin, that the faithful might worship their dead god.

But, today, these magnificent statues lie in toppled ruins all over the *"worker's paradise"* of Russia and Eastern Europe as the proletariat have vented their anger at the *"god"* of atheistic communism.

American democracy, however, is still alive and well. It is more than two centuries old and well into the third century. Unlike the French and Russian Revolutionists, Americans looked to the Sovereign Creator God of the universe, as revealed by Christ in the Bible, for solutions and help. The individual was responsible to God and the government responsible to the individual under God.

American democracy promises no utopia. It holds out no hope for the government as *"Big Brother"* to provide a heaven on earth. It guarantees only, the *"PURSUIT of happiness"* not *"happiness"*

CHAPTER 12

GEORGE WASHINGTON

A MAN OF FAITH

On February 22, 1732, into the home of Augustine and Mary Washington of Virginia, was born one of the most remarkable men to ever cross the stage of human history. He was America's first President and is lovingly referred to as the "Father of our country."

George Washington's father died when he was just eleven years old and as a result was unable to finish his formal education. He was raised primarily by his deeply devout, Christian mother, who had a profound effect upon him. Her letters and spiritual advice are preserved for us today in the Library of Congress. Whether little George chopped down a cherry tree and confessed to it, telling his father, *"I cannot tell a lie,"* I don't know. But the fact that this story has been handed down through the generations, surely speaks of the fact that George had a reputation for honesty and truthfulness.

George learned surveying in his teens and joined the Virginia militia as a young man, distinguishing himself as a junior officer in the French and Indian Wars. In one battle alone, four bullets passed through his coat and two horses were shot out from under him, yet he miraculously escaped harm. In describing the event, he spoke of "the *miraculous care of Providence.*"

As Commander-in-chief of the Continental Armies, he suffered from arthritus, tubercular pleurisy, dysentery, and frequent, recurring attacks of malaria. Small-pox left his face pock-marked, and *yet there is no record of his ever complaining about his lot.*

In 1776, after the Declaration of Independence was signed, Washington's first general order as chief of the newly organized Continental Army, was to call on every officer and man...to live and act as becomes a Christian soldier, defending the dearest rights and liberties of his country." *It is hard for me to believe, having spent a number of years in the Army, during World War II, but, in America's first Army—the rag tag, ill-equiped Army that won America's freedom and independence—it was a punishable offense to use profanity.*

In 1758, when Washington was a colonel in the Virginia militia, he established the post of chaplain to serve in each military regiment. Later he authorized a corps of chaplains to serve troops fighting in the Revolutionary War. Ministers were paid $20 a month and had the same privileges as a commissioned captain.

Washington believed that *"religion and public worship were essential to morale, both in civil and in military life."* He expected church attendance of his soldiers, and he regularly worshiped with his officers and men.

After leading America's first army to victory *over* the world's most powerful army and empire of that day, Washington was called on to preside over the Continental Congress that brought into being a Constitution that spelled out freedom to all.

And then, 9:00 a.m., April 30, 1789, Washington was inaugurated first President of these United States. He was greeted by a great, booming cheer from a sea of smiling faces that filled the streets of New York, as he walked out on the balcony of Federal Hall. Secretary of State, Samuel Otis, lifted the large, leather-covered Bible from its crimson, velvet cushion. Washington placed his left hand reverently upon the Bible, as he raised his right hand, to take the oath of office as President.

Repeating from memory the prescribed oath, he spontaneously added, "SO HELP ME GOD". Then, standing, tall and stately, with regal bearing, head and shoulders above the average man of his day, Washington, humbly and with moistening eyes, bowed reverently to kiss the Bible, he so loved and cherished, as God's Word.

In his inaugural address, Washington said, *"It would be peculiarly improper to omit in this first official act my fervent supplications to the Almighty Being who rules over the universe..."*

Washington and his guests were then escorted from Federal Hall through the crowded streets to St. Paul's Cathedral, in order to pray and *"hear divine services, performed by the Chaplain of Congress."*

When George Washington awakened on the first full day as first President of the United States—*the first nation of its kind in history*—the only job description he had, was the Constitution. He hired his personal staff, and appointed his four-man cabinet: Thomas Jefferson, Secretary of State: Alexander Hamilton, Secretary of the Treasury; Henry Knox, Secretary of War; and Edmund Randolph, Attorney General. He addressed the Congress; appointed the nation's ambassadors; and appointed the judges of the Supreme Court.

And though Martha Washington longed to retire to Mt. Vernon after their first four-year term, George consented to a second term, and was elected unanimously by the electoral college. And though the people might gladly have made him king, Washington refused to even consider the possibility.

How did George Washington manage to accomplish so much and so merit the undying love of America's people? He was a man of prayer and great faith. During his first year in office, he proclaimed Thursday, Nov. 26, 1789, a day for national Thanksgiving. He urged all Americans to *"unite in most humbly offering our prayers and supplications to the great Lord and Ruler of Nations..."*

A nephew of Washington and his private secretary, related to a friend that he had, *"accidentally witnessed Washington's private devotions in his library, both morning and evening; that on those occasions he had seen him in a kneeling posture with a Bible open before him, and that he believed such to have been his daily practice."*

John Marshall, chief justice of the Supreme Court, said about

Washington, *"Without making ostentatious professions of religion, he was a sincere believer in the Christian faith, and a truly devout man."*

John Schroeder in "Maxims of Washington" quotes him as follows: "*...reason and experience both forbid us to expect that National morality can prevail in exclusion of religious principle.. Of all the dispostions and habits which lead to political prosperity, RELIGION and MORALITY are INDESPENSIBLE supports. In vain would that man claim the tribute of Patriotism, who should labour to subvert these great PILLARS of human happiness..."*

That President George Washington was a devout believer in Jesus Christ, is easily demonstrated by a reading of his personal prayer book, *(written in his own handwriting)*, which was discovered in 1891 among a collection of his papers. Just one example is as follows: *"O most Glorious God...I acknowledge and confess my guilt....I have called on Thee for pardon and forgiveness of sins.. .Let me live according to those holy rules which Thou hast...prescribed in Thy holy Word; make me to know what is acceptable in Thy sight...increase my faith, and direct me to the true object, Jesus Christ, the Way, the Truth and the Life..."*

Two years after his farewell address to the nation, Washington, again a gentleman farmer, was caught in a snowstorm while out riding. He contracted a serious throat infection and was immediately treated with the most up-to-date medical science of his day. *Four times he was bled with leaches, and a preparation of dried beetles was placed on his throat.* But Washington grew weaker. On his deathbed he said to his physician: *"I die hard, but I am not afraid to go...I thank you for your attentions."*

At 10:00 p.m., December 14, 1799, George Washington stepped off the stage of history into the presence of the Savior he loved and served so faithfully all his life. Although, only 67 years old when he died, he had earned the right to be universally acclaimed as, FATHER OF OUR COUNTRY, for he was "<u>first in war, first in peace, and first in the hearts of his countrymen</u>."

CHAPTER 13

PRAYER CHANGES THINGS & PEOPLE

As the representatives met in Philadelphia to write the Constitution, they struggled for weeks making little progress. In fact, most were ready to give it up. They could not seem to agree on anything. *Tempers flared.*

But then 81 year old Benjamin Franklin rose to his feet as they were about to adjourn in confusion. He said, *"In the beginning of the contest with Britain, when we were sensible of danger, we had daily prayers in this room for Divine protection. Our prayers, Sirs, were graciously answered.. Have we now forgotten this powerful Friend?.. .I therefore beg leave to move that, henceforth, prayers imploring the assistance of Heaven and its blessing on our deliberation be held in this assembly every morning."* It was then, after Prayer, that America's miraculous Constitution came into being.

President Calvin Coolidge once said, *"America was born in a revival of religion."* He was referring to what historians call *"The Great Awakening."* The preaching of Jonathan Edwards and George Whitefield *changed* the moral and spiritual landscape of America before the Revolution and set in motion the forces that eventually brought America its political freedoms.

Most historians agree that Jonathan Edwards stands with Benjamin Franklin as *"one of the two outstanding minds in the America of the eighteenth century."* Edwards entered Yale at thirteen and graduated valedictorian at seventeen. He became President of Princeton and wrote numerous studies on theology, science and psychology, that are considered required reading for the truly educated even today.

It was the Sunday morning worship service at the Congregational meetinghouse in Enfield, Connecticut, July 8, 1741. The visiting preacher, Johathan Edwards, stepped up to the pulpit. He was just 36 years old. He wore a black robe with stiffly starched collar and a powdered wig.

With his Bible open on the pulpit and his *eyes fixed* upon his manuscript, (*held so close that the congregation could hardly see his face, because he was near-sighted*), he preached his famous sermon: "*Sinners in the Hands of an Angry God.*"

His voice did not shake the meeting house in great, pear-shaped tones. His arms *didn't gesture wildly.* He *didn't* pace or *perform.* He concluded his sermon, simply, with the invitation, *"let everyone that is out of Christ now awake and fly from the wrath to come."* Edwards was an *"intellectual"* and frowned upon emotional excesses.

An eyewitness, Stephen Williams, writes, that during the sermon, members cried out in great distress, *"What Shall I do to be Saved?...ye minister was obliged to desist...after Some time of waiting the Congregation were Still...and Amazing and Astonishing ye power o God was seen..."* Many were so moved, we are told, they caught hold of the back of the pews, lest they slip into the pit.

Although most of those who had settled the American colonies had come to America to escape the religious persecution that was rampant in Europe, many had grown lukewarm in their religious fervor. Self-indulgence, greed, drunkenness, and immorality became the norm. Churches became cold and formalistic. Edwards wrote that there were many, *"who scoffed and made a Ridicule of the Religion."*

During the next two years alone, some 25,000 to 50,000 people were added to the New England churches, out of a total population of only 300,000. The Great Awakening *changed* the moral and spiritual tone of New England. With the preaching of George Whitefield, and other preachers of the day, *The Great Awak-*

ening spread throughout the colonies, changing hearts and lives, and as a result, society, itself.

What was it that sparked such a great move of God following that worship service in Enfield? Was it Jonathan Edwards sermon, *"Sinners in the Hands of an Angry God."* No. He preached the same sermon in the church he pastored in Northampton a few weeks before with little response. What was the *secret ingredient* at Enfield that set such a blaze of religious fervor? *It was Prayer.*

Several women in the Enfield Congregation had become concerned about the moral conditions of the day and covenanted to pray, daily, for a spiritual revival. On the evening before that fateful day, these women, along with others of the church, met together and spent the whole night in agonizing prayer for their community. *The rest is history.*

George Whitefield was an *ornery* teen-ager. He loved to ridicule Christians, and preachers in particular. Yet, along with Jonathan Edwards, God used him mightily to bring revival not only to England, but America.

"My beloved brethren and sisters Give ear to the words of my mouth. I speak the message of the almighty." The crowd at the bar roared with laughter. *"Bravo, lad! Bravo,"* a stocky man shouted as he lifted his glass of brew. The young bar-keep, barely fifteen, was up to his favorite trick of mimicking Mr. Cole, the pastor of the Southgate Chapel in Gloucester, England.

Gloucester is a quaint, old, historic city, 114 miles west of London. It was near there, that William Tyndale was born in 1494. He was the first to translate the Bible into English, in order that *"every plough-boy might read it."* It was also at Gloucester that Robert Raikes started the first Sunday School in 1780.

And it was at Gloucester that one of the greatest preachers and evangelists the world has ever known was born. George Whitfield, was born Dec. 16, 1714. He grew up in an environment that, to say the least, was not conducive to morality and spirituality. His father died two years after he was born and left his mother with the responsibility of the family business, the Bell Inn. Tending bar left little time for her children, even though they lived at the Inn. In later life, Whitfield described his childhood, telling how he would lie, cheat, and steal money from his mother's pocket while she slept.

It is said that at the time, every sixth house was a saloon. One tavern boldly dispiayed a sign: *"Drunk for one penny, dead-drunk for twopence, clean straw for nothing!"* When the straw-covered cellar could accommodate no more the pavement outside would be thick with vomit and passed-out drunks.

The shows at the theatres were so vile and obscene that women who insisted on seeing the plays would wear veils or masks over their faces to hide their identity. Crime abounded. It was so unsafe, both in the city and the country-side, that no one dared venture out at night unless compelled to do so. Hold-ups and murders were so common that traveling alone was extremely dangerous.

And yet out of this environment came a man who not only helped to transform the moral and spiritual landscape of England but the American colonies as well. In fact, historians credit the religious Revival referred to as the Great Awakening in the 1700s with bringing about the political freedoms, we know as a nation. George Whitfield was a major force used of God in that awakening.

What was it that brought about such a change in this young bar-keep. He met John and Charles Wesley at Oxford, where he managed to work his way through by waiting on tables. He yearned for something that would satisfy the hungering of his heart. He had tasted of all the pleasures the world had to offer and knew them to be empty. He joined the *"Holy Club"* or *"Methodists"*. And yet, even though he fasted and prayed as religiously as the others, he still failed to find the peace and satisfaction he was looking for.

Then one day, Charles Wesley lent him a book called *"The Life of God in the Soul of Man."* The teachings of the book shone into his heart like rays of light. *"God showed me,"* Whitfield wrote later, *"that true religion was union of the soul with God, and Christ proved within us."*

He gave himself to incessant prayer. Night after night he groaned and agonized on his bed. He tried living on a starvation diet and giving almost all of his money to the poor. He wore coarse woolen gloves, a patched gown, and dirty shoes. Finally, his feverish seeking for union with God made him ill.

Then one day he remembered that Jesus' declaration of His thirst had come as he hung on the cross and almost finished. Young Whitefield suddenly threw himself down on his bed. *"I thirst! I thirst!"* he cried. Later he testified of what happened. *"Soon after this, I felt in myself that I was delivered from the burden and I knew what it was to truly rejoice in God as my Saviour."*

Barely a year later, Whitefield was preaching his *"new birth"* doctrine in London's largest churches. When the doors of the churches were closed to him, he preached in the fields with as many as thirty-thousand and more coming from all over England to hear him. He was just 26.

In 1739 he sailed for America where he helped spark and fan into flame the Great Awakening. Benjamin Franklin, who became a close friend of Whitefield, wrote: *"The multitudes of all sects and denominations that attended his sermons were enormous, and it was a matter of speculation to me, who was one of the number, to observe the extraordinary influence of his oratory on his hearers and how much they admired and respected him.*

"It was wonderful to see the change soon made in the manners of our inhabitants; from being thoughtless or indifferent about religion,...it seemed as if all the world were growing religious, so that one could not walk through the town in an evening without hearing psalms sung in different families of every street...Upon one of his arrivals from England at Boston, he wrote to me that he should come soon to Philadelphia but knew not where he could lodge when there. My answer was, 'You know my house; if you can make shift with its scanty accommodations, you will be most heartily welcome.'"

The first building at the University of Pennsylvania, was built at the instigation of Benjamin Franklin to hold the crowds that came to hear Whitefield preach. A statue of George Whitefield still stands on the campus.

In 1752 Whitefield wrote to Benjamin Franklin: *"As I find you growing more and more famous; in the world of letters I recommend to your unprejudiced study the mystery of the New Birth...I bid you, dear friend, remember that He before whose bar we must both soon appear has solemnly declared that without it we shall in no wise see His Kingdom."*

Though not known for his piety and orthodoxy in his early years, so influenced by the preaching of Whitefield was Franklin that he almost single-handedly enabled the American Constitution to be brought into existence. *Throughout America's history, in her darkest hours, as God's people prayed, God has brought healing to her land.*

It was Abraham Lincoln who proclaimed the first National Day of Prayer. He designated, Thursday, April 30, 1863. In 1857, moral conditions in America had reached an all time low. Slavery and all the horrors connected with it had been excused as an economic necessity in the South with little thought of the human suffering involved. Like the *Roe v Wade* decision about abortion and the rights of unborn babies, the *Dred Scott* decision declared slaves to be *non-persons* with their owners given the *"choice"* of whether they lived or died.

But Jeremiah Lanphier, started a prayer meeting in an upper room of the Dutch Reformed Church in Manhattan. He advertised it. Only six people (*from a population of one million*) showed up. But soon, they not only filled that Church, but the Methodist Church and every public building in downtown New York.

Famed newspaper editor, Horace Greeley, sent a reporter with horse and buggy, riding around the prayer meetings, to see how many men were praying. In one hour, he counted 6,100 men. *A landslide of prayer had begun.*

People began to be converted, finding a personal relationship with Christ, (*16,000 a week in New York City alone*). The movement spread throughout New England. Church bells brought people to prayer, morning, noon, and night. Churches around the country could not hold the overflowing crowds that came to worship. *It is believed by many historians, that it was this revival that eventually brought an end to slavery in America.*

In the early 1900s another revival broke out, that historians attribute to the praying of Ivy League students at Yale University. As they prayed, a spiritual awakening began to sweep across the campus and across the whole country. In Portland, Oregon, 240 department stores closed from 11 to 2 p.m. for prayer.

On the front page of the Denver Post, Jan. 20, 1905, appeared this headline. "ENTIRE CITY PAUSES FOR PRAYER".The article that followed read: *"For two hours at midday all Denver was held in a spell...The Spirit of the Almighty pervaded every nook.... thousands of men and women radiated this Spirit... the clear Colorado sunshine was made brighter by the reflected glow of the light of God shining upon happy faces..."*

The awakening swept across the Atlantic ocean to England, and Wales in particular, like a tidal wave. In Wales the social impact was astounding. During a five month period at the height of the revival, there were no rapes, no robberies, no murders, no embezzlements. Drunkenness was cut in half. The illegitimate birth rate dropped 44 percent within a year. The District Consuls held emergency meetings to discuss what to do with the excess number of police, since they had so little to do. *It sounds unbelievable, but it is a fact of history* "*If my people, which are called by my name, shall humble themselves and pray, and* seek *my face, and turn from their wicked ways, then will I hear from heaven, and will forgive their sin, and will heal their land."* (2 Chron. 7:14)

A number of years ago, the following appeared in the *Wall Street Journal:* "*What America needs...is a revival of religion, the kind that our fathers and mothers used to have; a religion that counted it good business to take time for family worship each morning right in the middle of the harvest, a religion that made men quit work a half hour earlier on Wednesday so the whole family could get ready to go to prayer meeting."*

Doctors are discovering that prayer can accelerate the healing process, whether it's the patient or others who do the praying. In one experiment a number of cardiac patients at San Francisco General Hospital were prayed for by a group of outsiders. The patients were not informed that they were being prayed for, but they still recuperated more quickly than patients in a control group.

Dr. Will Mayo of the world famed Mayo Clinic, said, *"I have seen patients that were dead by all standards…But I have seen a minister come to the bedside and do something for him that I could not do,… in defiance of medical knowledge and materialistic common sense, that patient LIVED!"*

Arthur Kornhaber, a psychotherapist who works with troubled adolescents, finds prayer a useful adjunct to conventional therapy. He goes so far as to say that *"to exclude God from psychiatric consultation is a form of malpractice."* Prayer has a very positive effect on marriage. Research indicates that couples who pray together tend to have a much higher satisfaction level than those who don't.

God says, *"Call unto me, and I will answer thee, and shew thee great and mighty things, which thou knowest not."* (Jer. 33:3) *And wonder of wonders, God is never too busy to hear our prayers. When we want to talk to the Lord, we never get a busy signal, nor are we put on hold. God is always there. "The eyes of the Lord are on the righteous, and His ears are open to their cry."* (Psalm 34:15)

CHAPTER 14

BILL OF RIGHTS

FREEDOM *"OF"* OR *"FROM"* RELIGION

For over 200 years Americans have enjoyed the blessed privilege to worship or not worship God, according to the dictates of their own conscience *without* interference from the State or an established, tax-supported, State Church.

It was with reverential awe that I stood some years ago in the pulpit of the historic First Baptist Church of Providence, Rhode Island, founded in 1638 by Roger Williams in his home. In 1636 Roger Williams was banished from Massachusetts because of his outspoken support of complete religious freedom. He lived among the Indians for a time and finally settled with others of like faith in the wilderness which became Rhode Island.

There, he established the first civil government on earth with *complete* religious freedom and separation of Church and State. The charter reads: *"... all men may walk as their consciences persuade them, every one in the name of his God..."*

Although the first settlers of America came to these shores to escape the persecution they had suffered at the hands of both the State and the established Church, most of the colonies in turn set up within their own borders one single denomination as an official, established church, supported by the taxation of all.

In Virginia, for example, by an edict of the civil authorities, every person in the Colony was required by law *"to repair to the* minister (Church of England) that their orthodoxy might be tested." For refusing, the offender was publicly whipped.

One preacher, Jeremiah Moore, was a special target of the establishment authorities. He was arrested for *unauthorized* preaching, and imprisoned. At Moore's trial, however, there came galloping up to his defense, none other than the famous lawyer and fiery orator, Patrick Henry. The one whose words, *"Give me liberty or give me death,"* inspired Americans to fight for liberty, fought for the liberty of Baptist preacher, Jeremiah Moore. In his impassioned plea before that court, Patrick Henry shouted, *"Great God, gentlemen, a man in prison for preaching the gospel of the Son of God!!"* Moore was released.

When Patrick Henry died, he had little to leave his family in the way of material wealth. His will read, *"...I have now disposed of all my property to my family. There is one thing more I wish I could give them and that is faith in Jesus Christ. If they had that and I had not given them one shilling, they would have been rich: and if they had not that, and I had given them all the world, they would be poor indeed."*

Another preacher among the many that were hauled off to prison for preaching without being authorized to do so by the State Church of Virginia was James Ireland. He would not be silenced, however, for he continued to preach through the bars of the small window of his jail cell. Crowds gathered to hear him. In that crowd, one day, was a teen age boy by the name of James Madison. James Madison from that time on became a crusader for absolute religious liberty.

After the original Constitution had been completed in 1787, fearing that liberty of conscience might not be sufficiently secured, the Baptists of Virginia sent a communication, dated August 8, 1789, to President George Washington proposing a Bill of Rights guaranteeing religious freedom. The President wrote in reply, *"If I could have entertained the slightest apprehension that the Constitution framed in the convention...might possibly endanger the religious rights of ecclesiastical society, certainly I would never have placed my signature to it..."*

Wheels began to turn, and one afternoon early in the first session of Congress all eyes turned toward a small man with sparse dark hair and piercing gray eyes. James Madison stood and announced: *"Mr. Speaker, I have the honor to present for the consideration of this body certain proposed amendments to the Constitution of the United States...Congress shall make no law respecting an establishment of religion, or prohibiting the free exercise thereof: or abridging the freedom of speech, or of the press, or of the right of the people peaceably to assemble..."*

The Bill of Rights had started on its way to adoption, and America became the first nation on earth to guarantee religious freedom. It was Sept. 25, 1789.

Clearly the First Amendment was not designed to restrict or censor out religion in the public sphere. The same Congress that wrote into the Constitution the Bill of Rights, also approved in 1789 the Northwest Ordinance which began, *"Religion, morality and knowledge being necessary to good government and the happiness of mankind, schools and the means of education (in religion, morality, and knowledge) shall forever be encouraged."*

President Washington who presided over the Constitutional Convention, took the oath of office with his hand on the Bible as has every President since. From the beginning of America's Judicial system, it has been the practice for witnesses to swear to tell the truth *"so help me God"* with their hand upon the Bible. Congress approved a Congressional Chaplain, and every session since has been opened with prayer. Military Chaplains have been an essential part of America's armed forces since the Revolution. *"One nation under God"* is in our pledge of allegiance to the flag, and *"In God we trust"* is on our currency.

The eighty-third Congress set aside a small room in the Capitol, just off the rotunda for the private prayer and meditation of members of Congress. The room's focal point is a stained glass window showing George Washington kneeling in prayer. Above the head of the Chief Justice of the Supreme Court are the *"Ten Commandments"*.

In spite of what some have been led to believe, an American does not lose his religious freedom when he steps onto public property. He can still pray, read his Bible and share his Faith with others. *It was the promoting of one religion over another by the government, the censoring and persecuting of others, and the taxation of all to support an established Church that prompted the Bill of Rights.*

Although it was risky, the framers of the Bill of Rights believed that *the common man had sense enough to discern truth from error and make up his own mind, as long as all beliefs were allowed free expression, even if they might not be considered "politically correct" by some.*

Russ Pulliam of the "Indianapolis News" writes: *"Those who think that religion ought to be kept out of public places should propose a constitutional amendment, declaring: 'Religion is dangerous to the public health and ought to be quarantined in the home and church', but",* he goes on to say, *"based on historical record, the Founding Fathers would vote "NO".*

Through the years, Christianity and its churches have flourished, as well as other religions. *Why?* Because the Bill of Rights guarantees a level playing field in the free market place of ideas and theologies.

James Madison, called the Father of the Constitution and the Bill of Rights, wrote, *"Belief in a God, all powerful and good is essential to the moral order of the world and to the hapiness of mankind."*

John Jay, appointed the first Chief Justice of the Supreme Court by George Washington, wrote, *"The real object of the First Amendment was not to advance infidelity by prostrating Christianity; but to exclude all rivalry among Christian sects and to prevent any national ecclesiastical extablishment which should give to the hierarchy the exclusive patronage of the national government."*

The Bill of Rights does not guarantee freedom *"from"* religion, as secularists contend, but freedom *"of"* religion, and *"the free excercise thereof."*

CHAPTER 15

A MISSION TO THE WORLD

From the beginning, American Christians have sought to share their Faith and the love of Christ with others. When the new American Congress met for the first time, its first act was to authorize the printing of 20,000 Bibles to be distributed to the American Indians. Evidently, America's founding fathers didn't believe it to be *"unconstitutional"* to do so.

The last words of Jesus to his apostles before ascending to His Father was the Great Commission. *"Go ye therefore, and teach all nations, baptizing them in the name of the Father, and of the Son, and of the Holy Ghost: Teaching them to observe all things whatsoever I have commanded you: and, lo, I am with you alway, even unto the end of the world."* (Matt. 28:19,20)

The Apostles were obedient to Jesus' command, spreading the gospel of Christ to the far corners of the known world. And down through the years of history others have followed their example.

In spite of horrible torture and persecution by the Roman government in an attempt to stamp it out, Christianity spread like wild-fire during the first few centuries after Christ until it had reached the outer limits of the Roman Empire and beyond. It had leaped across the channel to the British Isles and little independent churches and believers were everywhere.

In 200 A.D. Tertullian wrote: *"Parts of Britain were inaccessible to the Romans but have yielded to Christ."* For centuries the Druids had practiced in the wilds of savage Britain a religion of magic, mysteries, human sacrifices, and the worship of spirits in the trees, but Christ was dispelling the darkness.

Around 389 A.D. there was born into the home of Calpurnius, a deacon of the church of Bannavern, a small village in North Britain, Patrick Magonus Segatus. Calpurnius was a centurion and collector of taxes for the Roman government, and the wealthiest man in the village.

One day Patrick was playing near the seashore with two of his sisters when some Irish pirates carried them away, kicking and screaming, to their ships. Arriving in Ireland, Patrick stood in chains, dazed and trembling, on the slave block. Yesterday, he had been the pampered darling of the wealthiest family in town. Life had been easy and good. But, today, His new robe hung in tatters. He was a slave, the lowest of the low. Patrick was bought by the highest bidder and sent out into the fields to be a swineherd.

It was during the six years that he was a slave that he came to know Jesus personally as his Savior. Though Patrick had worshipped every Sunday at home, he had grown up with a placid indifference, taking it all for granted. But as a slave in Ireland, the gospel he had heard so often became real.

He wrote later, *"I was 16 years old, and knew not the true God; but in that strange land the Lord opened my unbelieving eyes, and, although late, I called my sins to mind, and was converted with my whole heart to the Lord my God...who consoled me as a father consoles his children."*

Miraculously, one night, Patrick was able to slip away from his captors and walked 200 miles to the far off port of Dublin. Finally, he reached the shores of Britain, and walking for a full month, arrived at his father's farm on the banks of the Solway.

How wonderful it was to be home, to be free, to luxuriate once more in the good things his father's wealth provided. But somehow the trappings of luxury and material things could not satisfy the gnawing that was in his heart. He was restless.

One night he had a dream in which he saw a man coming toward him walking through the mist. Suddenly it seemed that the room was full of light and a thousand voices calling to him in the music of the Gaelic tongue, *"Come, holy youth, and walk with us again."*

Patrick awoke with a start; with tears of compassion for the lost condition of those who had enslaved him. Now he knew why he had been so restless. God was calling him to go back to Ireland with the gospel to tell the people of Ireland of the faith he had found in Christ. His parents and friends tried to dissuade him. They thought him mad. He had no one to support him in his missionary efforts, only God. He wrote: *"It was not done of my own strength, it was God who overcame all."*

At last, after careful preparation and recruiting other Christians skilled in carpentry and other crafts to go with him to build churches in Ireland, he set sail. At the first place they set foot in Ireland, the natives drove them off with a barage of stones. The next place they stood their ground and Dichu, the native chieftain, listened when Patrick told him of Christ's love for him and how he died to save him from his sins. The chieftain, impressed with Patrick's courage and convicted by the Holy Spirit, responded. He was Patrick's first convert.

Dichu offered a wooden barn for a church. Peasants for miles around came to hear Patrick preach. They too received Christ. The good news of the love of Christ for the Irish quickly spread throughout the land.

Patrick finally had to challenge the Druid priests face to face. It was Easter eve, the eve of the most holy Druid ceremony and it was at Tara, home of Ireland's High-King, Loaghaire. The Druid's holy decree forbade any fire to be lit in all Ireland until a ceremonial flame was kindled in the court of the High-King.

That night, Patrick climbed a nearby hill and held a torch to a pile of brush and timber. Patrick waited King Loaghaire cried out in rage for Patrick to come down. As he strode down the hill, he sang, *"Of the Lord is salvation. Christ is salvation."* God touched the King's heart, and although he never abandoned his Druid worship, he granted Patrick permission to preach and gave him land

and lumber for churches. Patrick collected the people together in the fields by beating a drum and then preaching to them.

After many years of preaching and establishing churches in Ireland, Patrick at last penned his *"Confessions"* telling of his work. *"I'm a humble man,"* he wrote, *"a man with little education who dared to believe that God would give him wisdom...whatever tiny success was mine, or whatever I showed in accordance with God's will, I most truly believe that it was the gift of God."*

Patrick died, March 17, it is believed in the year 461 A.D. and was buried on the very spot where Dichu, his first convert, confessed faith in Christ. There are many legends about St. Patrick. Many are that, and nothing more. But one thing we know, St. Patrick was a real and living person who knew through personal experience a real and living Lord. He had a real and extraordinary love for the people of Ireland and through great sacrifice brought them the light of Christ's love. It's no wonder St. Patrick is honored by the people of that emerald isle, and in America we celebrate St. Patricks Day.

Having had a mother of Irish descent, whose favorite color was green, I have always felt that somehow it was sacrilegious not to wear something green on St. Patrick's Day. Even though her family came to America over 250 years ago, she always considered herself Irish. I guess you can take the family out of Ireland, but you can't take the Irish out of the family. Come to think of it, who would want to!

The modern missionary movement, which began in 1792 with William Carey of England, was sparked by the *"Great Awakening"* in America. Carey's zeal for taking the gospel of Christ to the whole world was set aflame by his reading of the *"Diary of David Brainerd"*.

"Oh, that I were a flame of fire in my Master's cause!" wrote David Brainerd in his diary. Brainerd had such intense compassion for souls, and was so earnest for their salvation that he said, *"I cared not where or how I lived, or what hardships I went through, so that I could but gain souls to Christ. While I was asleep, I dreamed of these things, and when I awoke the first thing I thought of was this*

great work. All my desire was for the conversion of the Indians, and all my hope was in God."

David Brainerd was engaged to the daughter of Jonathan Edwards, but died before they could be married.

He was converted during the Great Awakening under the preaching of Jonathan Edwards, and felt called of God to take the gospel to the Indians. Although dying at a young age, he was extremely successful in reaching the Indians for Christ. He lived in the wilderness, pitching his tent as close as possible to the Indian villages, praying that he might have opportunity to witness.

One day, tomahawks in hand, some Indians crept toward his tent. As they cautiously peered under the flap, their intention to kill was forgotten. There in the center of the tent was a man on his knees. As he prayed, a rattlesnake crossed his feet and paused in position to strike. But the snake did not strike. It lowered its head again and glided out of the tent.

Later, David Brainerd, found out why the Indians at the village received him with such honor as they did. He had expected that they would want to kill him. The reason for their change of heart was the report their comrades had brought of the marvelous thing they had seen. The Indians looked upon David Brainerd as a messenger from the Great Father, which he was.

October 2, 1792, 12 ministers, a student and a layman, met in Widow Wallis' house, known popularly as the "*Gospel Inn*" in Kettering, England. At the urging of a "*plodding*" Baptist preacher by the name of William Carey, they organized themselves together into a missionary society with a total of $100 in the treasury. The purpose—to preach the gospel of Christ to the whole world as Jesus had commanded in the Great Commission.

Carey had been christened as a baby in the Church of England, but had little interest in church. While still an apprentice shoe cobbler, he noticed, however, that a fellow apprentice, William Warr, seemed to really enjoy going to church and even reading his Bible. He, also, seemed to have an inner peace that Carey knew he didn't have.

Warr belonged to a tiny group of persecuted *"Dissenters."* One day he invited Carey to attend services with him, saying, *"What you need is to be born again."* Carey replies, *"Alright, I'll go to your church all three times this Sunday and leave off my lying and swearing."*

But peace didn't come. Something kept drawing him back, however, until one day as the preacher spoke about the reproach of following Christ, Carey writes, *"I had a desire to follow Christ...I felt ruined and helpless."* He received Christ as his personal Saviour—was born again—and experienced the peace he had been searching for.

After his conversion, William Carey could not learn enough about the Bible—even if it meant starving himself to buy precious books. One of these books was the *"Diary of David Brainerd"*. It set his heart on fire to take the gospel to those in foreign lands, who had never had opportunity to hear it.

In 1781 Carey opened his own cobbler's shop. He never sat down to work without a book before him. We picture him with his leather apron sitting at his workbench—2 or 3 nails in his mouth—between strokes of his hammer, glancing at the book before him. When he was old and world-famous he told his nephew, *"If anyone writes about my life they can give me credit for being a "Plodder."* Carey was poor, but he could plod.

On August 10, 1786, William Carey was ordained a Baptist minister. A few weeks later he was present at a ministers' meeting at Northampton. At the meeting, an older minister suggested one of the group name a topic for general discussion. Carey rose and hesitantly suggested, *"Whether or not the Great Commission is binding upon us today to go and teach all nations."*

Before another could speak, the moderator soundly rebuked Carey. *"Sit down, young man. When God pleases to convert the heathen, He will do it without your aid or mine."*

But finally at long last, in spite of the resitance of so many, William Carey's persistent *"plodding"* resulted in the launching of a movement 200 years ago that has inspired thousands upon thousands of dedicated missionaries from almost every denomination in America to carry the gospel of Christ to the far corners of the earth, not by force but demonstrations of love.

Carey, himself, was the first to go. After five months at sea, he and his family arrived in India. Threat of arrest by Calcutta authorities forced them into the interior through tiger-haunted swamps. But the plodder continued to plod. He translated the Bible into the four languages of India. He put out the first newspaper ever printed in an Oriental language.

Carey fought vigorously against the caste system, racism, abortion and infanticide. A sick baby was thought to be bewitched and so was left exposed to the elements to die. Sati (Suttee), *burning of Hindu widows upon the funeral pyre of the dead husband*, was another practice that burdened him. He is known in India as the *"father of education,"* having started India's first university and even gave Bengalis their written language.

After 41 years in his beloved India, the world renown, former shoemaker, who made the Bible available and readable to 300 million people in their own languages, whispered on his deathbed, *"What hath God wrought! When I am gone say nothing about Dr. Carey—speak about Dr. Carey's Saviour."*

After his death Calcutta newpapers joined Christian leaders around the world in lauding his greatness. On his gravestone was chiseled his life motto: *"Expect great things from God; attempt great things for God."*

For over 200 years the overwhelming majority of all Protestant Missionaries have come from America. One of America's first missionaries was Adoniram Judson who went out to preach the gospel in Burma. For seven heartbreaking years, he labored and suffered hunger and privation without winning one soul. He was thrown into prison and subjected to incredible torture and mistreatment. As a result, he carried the ugly marks made by the chains and iron shackles which cruely bound him.

Upon his release, he asked for permission to go to another province to preach the gospel. The ruler denied his request, saying, "*My people are not fools enough to listen to anything a missionary might say, but I fear they might be impressed by your scars, and turn to your religion.*" Because of Adoniram Judson's willingness to sacrifice himself for the cause of Christ, eventually, great multitudes of the Burmese people did accept the Christ that he preached.

In 1956, the world recoiled in shock with the news that five American missionaries had been speared to death in the Ecuadorian jungles by Auca Indians, reported to be the most savage tribe on earth. Their broken, mutilated bodies lay lifeless on a strip of white sand, deep in the Ecuadorian rain forest. The story quickly spread through every major wire service and newspaper. It was covered in detail by Life Magazine.

It seemed to the world like the tragic end to the broken dreams of some overzealous religious fanatics and a terrible waste of human life. Five young missionary wives were left widows, nine children had become fatherless. All because five young men in the prime of life were willing to give their lives, if need be, to carry the gospel to a tribe of Stone Age killers in Ecuador.

They and their families had prayed for God's direction. Each one of them had the assurance that God was leading and yet before they could get even one word of the gospel to these Auca Indians, all were dead.

And yet, today, through their example and the continued efforts of these men's wives and the miraculous power of God, everyone of the ten Auca Indians, that killed those missionaries that awful day, have become Christians, along with great numbers of the Auca tribe and many of the neighboring tribes.

CHAPTER 16

AN EDUCATED CITIZENRY NEEDED

America was founded by ordinary men and women who became extraordinary as they were profoundly influenced by the Bible and the teachings of Christianity.

To deny this is to deny history. The values which Christianity taught of goodness and self-control, of honesty and hard work, of diligence and sharing, of liberty within the context of responsibility and hard work are what made our country great.

Realizing the importance of education in passing on to their children and future generations their values and love for freedom, our pilgrim forefathers set up a school system, not just for those that could afford to pay tuition to private schools but tax-supported schools for the common man. In 1647, five years after establishing the Massachusetts Bay Colony, an ordinance was passed which marked the beginning of the U.S Public School system.

The Bible was put in the center of the curriculum. The encyclopedia Americana states, *"The puritans...were determined that children should receive sufficient education to insure their ability to read the Bible and to participate in religious services."* Passages from the Bible were used to teach reading and writing in those early colonial grammar schools.

The *"New England Primer"* contained 26 rhymes depicting Christian teachings, one for each letter in the alphabet. The first rhyme was *"In Adam's Fall, We Sinned All"* and illustrates why it was called the *"Little Bible"* of New England. This primer also contained the Lord's Prayer, The Apostles' Creed, the Ten Commandments, and The Duty of Children Towards Their Parents.

In 1836 William McGuffey published his first of a series of *"McGuffey Readers,"* that were filled with quotes from the Bible and emphasis on Judeo-Christian values. For over three-quarters of a century the *McGuffey Reader* and dedicated public school teachers *taught* America's children how to read and spell.

Noah Webster, friend of George Washington and Benjamin Franklin, pioneer educator, political writer, lecturer, and compiler of the American Dictionary of the English Language had this to say about education: *"To give children a good education in manners, arts and science, is important; to give them a religious education is indispensable; and an immense responsibility rests on parents and guardians who neglect these duties."* About the Bible, Webster said: *"The Bible should be the standard of language as well as of faith."*

The framers of the Constitution and their descendents, in their *"ignorance",—not realizing, of course, that it was "unconstitutional"*—for 200 years of our history as a nation, placed God, the Bible, and the life and teachings of Jesus at the heart of education in the United States. *Upon these strong spiritual foundations, the greatest public educational system in the history of the world was built.*

For the first 150 years, education in America and the Christian faith were inseparable. The Bible served as the standard by which all other truth was measured. The life and teachings of Jesus were at the heart of the curriculum. The framers of the Constitution were products of this Christ-centered and Bible-centered education.

Not only did the founding fathers of America set up a public school system to pass on to their children the values they held so dear as revealed in the Bible; they established schools of higher education, primarily to train ministers to preach the gospel. Eighty-eight of the first 100 colleges founded in the colonies prior to the Revolution, except the University of Pennsylvania—were established by some branch of the Christian church.

Even at the University of Pennsylvania, the Methodist evangelist, George Whitefield, played a prominent part. The first building of the present university was built for the purpose of accommodating the crowds which wanted to hear Whitefield preach—a decision of Benjamin Franklin and other supporters. A statue of Whitefield stands on that campus today. Every so-called Ivy league College in the East was established primarily to train ministers of the Gospel and to evangelize the eastern seaboard.

The first school of higher learning founded in America was Harvard in 1636. A pamphlet written in 1643 following the graduation of its first class and its words etched over its gates today describes in detail the history, purpose, and plan of Harvard in those early years:

"After God had carried us safe to New England, and wee had builded our houses, provided necessaries for our liveli-hood, rear'd convenient places for Gods worship, and setled the Civill Government: One of the next things we longed for, and looked after was to advance Learning and to perpetuate it to Posterity; dreading to leave an illiterate Ministery to the Churches, when our present Ministers shall lie in the Dust. And as wee were thinking and consulting how to effect this great Work, it pleased God to stir up the heart of one Mr Harvard (a godly Gentleman and a lover of Learning ...) towards the erecting of a Colledge, and all his library."

Some of the requirements for enrollment were: *"Let every Student be plainly instructed and earnest pressed to consider well the maine end of his life and studies is to know God and Jesus Christ which is eternall life, John 17:3 and therefore to lay Christ in the bottome, as the only foundation of all sound knowledge and Learning. And seeing the Lord only giveth wisdom, Let every one seriously set himself by prayer in secret to seek it of him".*

Among those who laid their lives on the line in signing the Declaration of Independence, and brought into being our beloved Constitution were some notable graduates of Harvard; John Adams, John Hancock, Samuel Adams, James Otis, and Joshiah Quincy. Each of these men faithfully subscribed to and followed these early requirements for enrollment.

Yale was founded in 1701 by ten Congregational ministers with the requirement, *"That the said Rector shall Cause the Scriptures Daily... morning and evening to be read by the Students at the times of prayer in the School..."* All professors and students had to subscribe to the Westminster Confession of Faith. Among the graduates of Yale in those early years that contributed so much to the freedoms that we know were the educator and author of the *dictionary,* Noah Webster, and the patriot, Nathan Hale, who just before being hanged by the British said, *"I only regret that I have but one life to lose for my country."* Timothy Dwight, president from 1795 to 1817, advised the class of 1814: *"Christ is the only, the true, the living way of access to God. Give up yourselves therefore to him..."*

When King's College, now Columbia University, opened in 1754, the following was part of an advertisement published for the school: *"The chief thing that is aimed at in this college is to teach and engage children to know God in Jesus Christ."*

Brown University was chartered as Rhode Island College, in 1764 by the Baptist descendants of Roger Williams, *"to train ministers and to educate youth properly in the Christian faith."* Roger Williams founded the first Baptist church in America at Providence, Rhode Island, and the first place in America with separation of church and state.

Princeton College was founded in 1746 by Presbyterian clergymen during the spiritual awakening that was then sweeping the colonies. It insisted that the faculty be *"convinced of the necessity of religious experience for salvation."* John Witherspoon, first president of Princeton, was a signer of the Declaration of Independence. Early Princeton graduates include James Madison (*called the father of the Constitution*), Henry Lee, and six members of the first United States Congress.

William and Mary College, founded in Virginia in 1691 was established *"that the Christian faith might be propagated."* Among its early graduates were Thomas Jefferson, James Monroe, George

Wythe, and John Marshall, Chief Justice of the U. S. Supreme Court.

It was a very specially dedicated public school teacher, daughter of a Presbyterian minister, that instilled in me a love of learning and was instrumental in my starting to Sunday School and finding Christ as my personal Savior, when just a 10-year-old boy. Some day when I meet her in heaven, I want to tell her how much she influenced my life.

There is a story told about a public school teacher that beautifully illustrates the tremendous influence a teacher may have in the life of a pupil.

It was her first year as a fourth-grade teacher. *"I would tell the children, 'I want you to know that I haven't any favorites. You are each individually important to me.'"*

She said, *"As much as I would have liked, it wasn't totally true. That year, Bobby Lindel was in my class and to be brutally honest, I disliked him. He would sit slouched in his seat, and glare at me defiantly. I considered him a hopeless case. He just refused to study, and I marked his test papers with an 'F' with relish.*

After some time she pulled out Bobby's school records to see how he had done in the lower grades. The notations were heartrending. *"First grade, Bobby is a bright boy, capable of learning, but seems to be troubled. Second grade, Bobby's mother is terminally ill; her illness has devastated Bobby. Third grade, Bobby's mother died. The notations show that his father is indifferent to him. He will fail if something isn't done."*

"When I'd finished reading," she said, *"my cheeks were wet with tears. Here was a little boy who desperately needed someone to care. I determined to be that someone. I gave Bobby the special attention and affection he so badly needed."*

She lost track of Bobby when he left her class. But one day, several years later, she received a short note from him. It read, *"I graduated from high school. I was second in my class. I wanted you to be the first to know."*

And then a number of years later, she received a second letter from Bobby. *"I have just finished medical school. I graduated first in my class. Robert Lindel, M.D."*

"P.S.—I am getting married on the 16th. Since you are all the family I have (dad died last year), would you honor me at the wedding by sitting in the pew reserved for my mother? Love, Bobby."

One of the world changing influences that grew out of the evangelical revival of the 1700s was the Sunday School. It was started by Robert Raikes, editor and publisher of the Gloucester Journal He grew up in the same city as the evangelist, George Whitefield.

Influenced by the preaching of Whitefield and the Wesleys, he became a crusading editor and sought to bring about a number of social reforms in England. He exposed prison abuses and other social evils, such as child labor and slavery.

In that day many children at a very young age were forced to work some times as much as 60 hours a week in the factories and sweat shops of England. The only time off was on Sunday afternoons. These children, not able to receive any schooling and tending to roam the streets and get into trouble when they were off, burdened Raikes heart.

He engaged several women, who taught schools in the neighborhood, to teach these poor, dirty, undisciplined boys and girls how to read. The Bible was their text book and they held class on Sunday afternoon. Raikes paid the teachers out of his own pocket one shilling (25c) a day for their services. He even gave the children a penny for attending and soon had a large number of children in classes all over the city. He distributed books among them: gave them advice, and settled their quarrels.

Stealing, vandalism, and gang violence was so drasticly reduced by these Sunday Schools that the police took notice and others began to follow his example and Sunday schools blossomed all over England. In just five years there were more than 250,000 children enrolled in Sunday school.

John Wesley suggested that the teacher's should be volunteers and for 200 years since, dedicated Christians, both men and women, have sacrificed out of love, their time, talents, knowledge, effort, and means to teach God's Word to spiritually needy boys and girls, men and women.

One of the oldest Christian organizations in the U. S., still in existence, is the American Sunday School Union. A group of Philadelphia citizens founded the organization in a school room at Forth and Vine Streets on May 13, 1817. Its prime mover was Dr. Benjamin Rush, signer of the Declaration of Independence and the most eminent American physician of his generation. Among its original vice presidents was Bushrod Washington, nephew of George Washington. Also among its early officers was John Marshall, Chief Justice of the U. S. Supreme Court. Another long-time vice president was Pennsylvania Governor, John Pollock who, as director of the U. S. Mint in Philadelphia, first inscribed on our coins the motto, *"In God We Trust."*

But one of the movements most illustrious figures, was a man who served as manager and vice-president of the American Sunday School Union from its inception until his death 18 years later. During the War of 1812, he found himself held captive aboard a British ship outside the city of Baltimore, near Fort McHenry. He watched *"the rockets' red glare, the bombs bursting in air."* Then Francis Scott Key wrote *"The Star Spangled Banner!"*

Tens of thousands of Sunday Schools have been organized across America following the migration west from the Appalachian cabins to the frontier towns of the wild, wild west.

A study made of 600 juveniles incarcerated for the adult crimes of robbery, rape, and murder revealed the following startling facts. Six out of ten had fathers or mothers who drank to excess. Three out of four were permitted by parents to come and go as they pleased. Seven out of ten had homes where no group or family activities were enjoyed. And ten out of ten never attended Sunday school. Not one out of the 600.

Someone asked John Wanamaker, a Presbyterian layman and millionaire merchant of Philadelphia, *"How do you get time to run a*

Sunday school with over 4,000 members, in addition to your multi-million dollar business of your stores, your work as U. S. Postmaster General, and other obligations."

Instantly, Mr. Wanamaker replied: "Why, the Sunday School is my business! All other things are just "things". Forty-five years ago I decided that God's promise was sure: 'Seek ye first the kingdom of God, and his righteousness: and all these things shall be added unto you.'"

He said, "I have made large purchases of property in my lifetime...and the buildings and property I own represent a value of approximately 20 billion dollars. But it was as a boy in the country, at eleven years of age, that I made my biggest purchase. In a little mission Sunday School, I bought from my teacher a small red leather Bible. The Bible cost me $2.75—which I paid in small installments as I saved. 'That was my greatest purchase, for that Bible made me what I am today.'"

After that statement, the New York Herald Tribune captioned its write up thus: "LATER DEALS IN MILLIONS CALLED SMALL COMPARED WITH BUYING HOLY WRIT AT ELEVEN."

CHAPTER 17

WHAT GOD'S *"AMAZING GRACE"* CAN DO

The story is told of a little known consulting firm which specializes in analyzing candidates for management positions in various organizations. They recently uncovered some old files which throw some interesting light on what some might consider essential skills and abilities for Christian service. The report reads:

To: Jesus of Nazareth:
Regarding: 12 candidates for management positions
Dear Sir:

Thank you for submitting the resumes of the twelve men you have picked for positions in your new organization. All of them have now taken our battery of tests, and we have not only run the results through our computer, but also arranged personal interviews with each of them with our psychologist and vocational aptitude consultant.

It is the staff opinion that most of your nominees are lacking in background, education and vocational aptitude for the type of enterprise you are undertaking. They do not have the team concept. We would recommend that you continue your search for persons of experience in managerial ability and proven capability.

Simon Peter is emotionally unstable, and given to fits of temper. Andrew has absolutely no qualities of leadership. The two brothers, James and John, place personal interest above company loyalty and show tendencies of paranoia toward outsiders. Thomas demonstrates a questioning attitude that would tend to undermine morale. We feel that it is our duty to tell you that Matthew, the former tax collector, has been blacklisted by the Greater Jerusalem Better Business Bureau. James, the son of Alphaeus. and Thaddeus definitely have radical leanings, and they both register a high score on the manic scale. One of the candidates, however, shows a great potential. He is a man of ability and resourcefulness, meets people well, has a keen business mind and has contacts in high places. He is highly motivated, ambitious and responsible. We recommend Judas Iscariot as your first vice president and comptroller of company funds.

Sincerely yours,

Jesus spent an entire night in prayer before he chose the Twelve: Three of them are recorded as having uttered only a single sentence. Six did not say anything the gospel writers thought worthy of recording. Yet, Jesus, the Son of God, chose these very ordinary men to undertake the most important enterprise in the world.

All of the apostles had glaring faults and weaknesses, and yet it was said of them that they turned the world upside down. In spite of the paganism and the tremendous persecution they faced, in just a few years, by 300 A.D. half of the known, civilized world had become Christian.

Why were such ordinary men able to do so much, with so little, against such odds? They had seen the resurrected Christ and their lives had been transfomed by His resurrcction power. They were set on fire by a passionate love for Christ and those He died for on the Cross of Calvary. They were endued with a power that only an omnipotent God could give in the person of the Holy Spirit

It is not what we have to offer to God, but what God can do through us that counts in Christian service. *"For ye see your calling, brethren, how that not many wise men after the flesh, not many mighty, not many noble, are called; but God hath chosen the foolish things of the world to confound the wise; and God hath chosen the weak things of the world to confound the things which are mighty...That no flesh should glory in his presence... that, according as it is written, He that glorieth, let him glory in the Lord."* (1 Cor. 1:26-31).

John Newton was the son of a seaman in the British Navy. By age 23, John had become the captain of his own ship. Publically flogged and disgraced for having lost his ship at sea, Newton became bitter toward God and man. He went to Africa to work for a man who dealt in slaves, where he, too, became a slave. He escaped, however, and became the captain of his own slave ship, which, to show his contempt for Christianity, he named it, *"Jesus."*

It was past midnight, March 21, 1748. John Newton was sound asleep in his cabin. Suddenly a huge wave crashed against the wooden ship. John was thrown out of his bunk and onto the floor, where he landed with a splash. To his alarm, John saw his cabin was quickly filling up with water! The ship was breaking apart from a violent storm that had come up suddenly.

In desperation, John Newton—the atheist, the libertine, the slave trader—cried out, *"Oh God, help me! Don't let me die! Oh, God, I know what a terrible sinner I am. I know that I don't deserve Your mercy, but I'm begging You to please take pity on me. Forgive me for my sins, and I promise You that I'll be different from now on! Please God, spare my life!"*

The storm began to ease as suddenly as it had come and the sea became calm. Newton now was overwhelmed with a consuming desire to know more about the One he had been so bitter toward and cursed so often, Jesus Christ. He spent day after day reading a Bible one of the sailors had brought along.

As John Newton read and prayed and confessed his sins, asking God's forgiveness, he experienced the *"Amazing Grace"* of Jesus as the light and joy and peace of God's salvation burst upon his soul.

God called him to preach at age 40. He was accepted as an Anglican clergyman and became curate at Olney in

Buckinghamshire. It was during the years he served there that he wrote the hymn for which he is best remembered: *"Amazing Grace."*

"Amazing grace, how sweet the sound, That saved a wretch like me! I once was lost, but now am found, Was blind, but now I see."

Writing out of his own, experience, Newton penned the third stanza: *"Through many dangers, toils, and snares, I have already come: 'Tis grace hath bro't me safe thus far, And grace will lead me home."*

Looking forward expectantly to the future, he wrote the last stanza: *"When we've been there ten thousand years, Bright shining as the sun, We've no less days to sing God's praise Than when we first begun."*

Through the influence of John Newton, William Wilberforce, succeeded in persuading the Parliament to ban the slave trade in England. It was through the Abolitionist Movement, composed, primarily, of Evangelical Christians, inspired by John Newton, that the slaves in America were, eventually, *"emancipated"* by Abraham Lincoln.

As Newton lay upon his deathbed, a young clergyman came to see him and expressed regret at the prospect of losing so eminent a laborer in the Lord's vineyard. Newton replied, *"I'm going on before you, but one day you will follow. When you arrive—if you enquire of me—I'll be sitting at the feet of the thief whom Jesus saved in His dying moments on the cross!"*

Although a distinguished and highly respected clergyman at the time, Newton felt with Paul that he could only class himself among the chiefest of sinners who have been saved through the *"Amazing Grace"* of Jesus.

"For by grace are ye saved through faith; and that not of yourselves; it is the gift of God, Not of works, lest any man should boast." (Eph. 2:8-9)

CHAPTER 18

LIBERATED WOMEN
WHO MADE THEIR LIFE COUNT

Susanna Wesley was born in London, Feb. 20, 1669, the youngest of 25 children born to Dr. Samuel Annesley. It was the year Rembrandt died and Stradivari created his famous violin. Three years before, a plague swept through the city of London, killing thousands, and a great fire destroyed three-quarters of the city.

Susanna's father, Dr. Annesley, was born in 1620, the same year the Pilgrims landed on Plymouth Rock. He was for years, vicar of St. Giles Church in London. There, the Dissenters, John Milton, author of *"Paradise Lost"* and John Foxe, author of *"Foxe's Book of Martyrs"* are buried. Because Dr. Annesley was also a Dissenter from the State supported and only authorized Church of England, along with 2,000 other ministers (*Baptist, Presbyterian, Independents, and others*) he was driven from his pulpit and spent a time in prison.

Susanna grew up in London with the Dissenter, Daniel Defoe, author of *"Robinson Crusoe"*. Expected to spend as much time reading the Bible as in play, she learned her Bible well. She would pray daily as a young girl, *"Dear God, guide me. Make my life count."* But God's answer seemed to be: *"Wait"*. So Susanna waited. And in the meantime, she married the young poet and minister, Samuel Wesley in 1689.

Samuel Wesley worked his way through Oxford as a *"servitor"*. A servitor waited on other students, shining their shoes, making their beds, carrying their books, tutoring, etc. He was a *"pauper scholaris"*. When he graduated, he was ordained in the Church of England.

Life in the rectory was not easy. There was never enough money to feed and clothe the family properly. Twice their house burned. Through it all, Susanna devoted herself to her children—nineteen were born, but only seven lived to maturity. She spent one hour each day shut up with God alone in her room, praying for her children. She was very methodical, and set down rules to follow in her mothering. She set aside a special time each day to be with each child individually. She taught them to respect and love their father, as she did, by setting the example.

Discipline was strict, but she was very patient with the children. One time, her husband said, *"I marvel at your patience! You have told that child the same thing twenty times!"* Susanna looked fondly at the child and said, *"Had I spoken the matter only nineteen times, I should have lost all my labor."*

Susanna died in 1742. Her final request was: *"Children, as soon as I am released, sing a psalm of praise to God."* At the time, all of her living children were believers. She was buried in Bunhill Fields—the Westminster Abbey of Dissenters. Near her grave are those of Isaac Watts, Daniel Defoe, John Bunyan and a host of others who gave their lives for the Word.

The influence of Susanna Wesley continued to burn within the hearts of her sons. John and Charles Wesley became the founders of Methodism and through the Wesleyan Revival, (*that swept through England and America*) brought spiritual awakening and moral reformation, just when it seemed there was no hope. Charles wrote 6,000 hymns and preached until he was past 80. John continued his ministry into his 87th year.

Four days before his passing, he wrote a final letter to the Christian patriot, William Wilberforce, who was fighting slavery in the House of Commons. In the letter he included the lines, *"Go on, in the name of God and in the power of His might, till even American slavery shall vanish before it."*

Susanna's prayer that *"her life might count"* was answered beyond her wildest dreams. She found complete fulfilment in being, *"just a mother"*.

Three of Susanna Wesley's sons earned degrees at Oxford. All were excellent scholars and earned their own way. They were much disturbed, however, by the extremely low morals of the students. Drinking, gambling, idleness, and loose living were common. Samuel, the oldest, became a King's Scholar and went on to teach at Westminster the rest of his life. John and Charles, while at Oxford, organized a little group of students, soon to be known as the *"Holy Club."* Learning the value of method from their mother, there was a certain time for prayer, for fasting, for studying the Bible, for distributing alms, for visiting prisoners, for group discussions, for taking communion, and so on. Because of these methods, members of the *"Holy Club"* were sneered at as being *"Methodists"*.

After graduating from Oxford and being ordained in the Church of England, John and Charles Wesley set sail, Oct. 14, 1735, for America to do missionary work in Georgia.

During the third month at sea their ship, the *"Simmonds"* was caught in a violent storm.. John wrote in his journal, *"The winds roared about us. The ship not only rocked...with the utmost violence, but shook and jarred with so unequal, grating motion, that one could not but with great difficulty keep one's hold of anything, nor stand a moment without it. Every ten minutes came a shock from the stern or side of the ship, which would think would dash the planks to pieces."*

The ship lurched crazily as it inched its way through twenty-foot-high waves in the Atlantic. A wall of water burst across the deck, split the mainsail of the eighteenth-century sailing vessel, and sloshed into the living quarters. The Reverend John Wesley shuddered in fear. Several Englishmen around him screamed. But when he glanced at a group of Moravians, he marveled that they were calmly singing a psalm. *"Heavy-minded and dull- witted folk,"* he thought.

When the seas had calmed, Wesley edged up to their leader.

"Were you not afraid in the storm?" he inquired. *"No. The Lord is on our side. We do not fear death."*

The next day the Moravian pastor, Spangenberg, had a question for the English minister. *"Friend Wesley, do you know Jesus Christ?"* he inquired. *"I know that He is the Saviour of the world,"* the dignified Englishman replied blandly. *"But can you tell me if He has saved you?"* Wesley was plainly flustered. *"I hope so,"* he answered uneasily.

The pastor's emphasis on *"you"* startled John. Didn't the man know that he had an Oxford degree, that he was an ordained priest, the son of an ordained priest, and ardent student of the Bible, and a missionary.

John Wesley was on his way to Georgia to evangelize the Indians. But before he was to find peace, himself, he was to wail, *"I came to Georgia to convert the Indians, but oh, who shall convert me? I have but a fair summer religion."* His *"fair summer religion"* failed to move the indifferent English colonists, much less the pagan Indians. He returned to England after two years, his missionary journey a failure.

Who were these Moravians, that so impressed John Wesley with their confident assurance and peace in the midst of storm. The Moravian Church grew out of the evangelical preaching of John Huss of Prague, Czechoslovakia, then Moravia. He sought to restore the Christianity of the New Testament with emphasis on the necessity of being *"born again"* through faith in Christ alone without works of any kind.

John Huss was burned at the stake on his birthday, July 6, 1415. When he heard his sentence pronounced, he fell to his knees and prayed, *"Lord Jesus, forgive my enemies."* When chained to the stake, he prayed, *"In Thee, O Lord, do I put my trust: let me never be ashamed."* He died smiling, singing the praises of God.

Back in England, John Wesley's sister, Kezzy, had a breakthrough experience of the new birth. Her feeling of assurance was so profound and so visible that Charles was inspired to write one of his greatest hymns: *"Love divine, all love excelling, Joy of Heaven,* to earth come down, Fix in us Thy humble dwelling, All thy faithful mercies crown."

Following Kezzy's *"conversion"*, Charles had his own encounter with the Lord. It was in Little Britain, a short street in London that right-angles Aldersgate.It was May 21, and was the result of the witnessing of a *"poor ignorant mechanic, who knew nothing but Christ."*

Three days later, feeling that he had never really been converted, John Wesley concentrated on studying the New Testament. To his amazement, he learned that the conversion experience was almost always an instantaneous one. Finally, convinced that simple faith was the answer, he resolved in his own words to renounce *"all dependence in whole or in part, upon my own works or righteousness."*

But pray as he would, nothing seemed to happen. Then at about five in the morning on Wednesday, May 24, 1738, he opened his Greek New Testament to 2 Peter 1:4. There, he read: *"Whereby are given unto us exceedingly great and precious promises; that by these ye might be partakers of the divine nature."* Afterward, just as he left the house, he read the words of Jesus: *"Thou art not far from the kingdom of God"* (Mark 12:34).

He writes in his journal: *"In the evening I went very unwillingly to a society in Aldersgate Street, where one was reading Luther's preface to the Epistle to the Romans. About a quarter till nine, while he was describing the change which God works in the heart through faith in Christ, I felt my heart strangely warmed, I felt that I did now trust in Christ, alone, for salvation: and an assurance was given me, that he had taken away my sins, even mine, and saved me from the law of sin and death."*

Many years before a man named Nicodemus came *to Jesus, saying, we know that thou art a teacher come from God: for no man can do these miracles that thou doest, except God be with him."* (Jn 3:2).

Nicodemus was schooled in the Scriptures, a keeper of the law, and a highly respected religious leader of the day. Like John Wesley, he realized that there was something missing in his life.

Jesus, seeing Nicodemus' sincerity and his need, answered him: *"Except a man be born again, he cannot see the kingdom of God."* (Jn 3:3) Only in Christ is there true liberty. *"If the Son set you free, ye shall be free, indeed."* (John 8:36)

One of the most liberated of women was the beloved hymn writer, Fanny Crosby. She was born in Putnam County, New York, March 24, 1820. When she was only six weeks old she developed a minor eye inflammation and the doctor's careless treatment left her blind. The doctor who destroyed her sight never forgave himself and moved from the area, but Fanny Crosby was free of any ill will toward him.

"If I could meet him now," she once wrote, *"I would say, 'Thank you, thank you.'—over and over again—for making me blind."* In fact, she claimed that if she could have her sight restored, she would not attempt it. She felt that her blindness was God's gift to her so that she could write songs for his glory. *"I could not have written thousands of hymns,"* she said, *"if I had been hindered by the distractions of sight."*

Fanny was greatly influenced by her mother and grandmother (*her father died when she was very young*). When the family moved to Connecticut, a neighbor, Mrs. Hawley, read to her from the Bible and taught her Bible stories.

It seems unbelievable, but by the time Fanny was 10 years old, she could recite the first four books of the Old Testament and the four Gospels! Her mother enrolled her in the famous Institution for the Blind in New York City. She proved an excellent student in everything except arithmetic. One of her first poems read, *"I loathe, abhor, it makes me sick, To hear the word Arithmetic!"*

It was on November 20, 1850, that Fanny Crosby walked the aisle at a revival meeting being held at the Broadway Tabernacle Methodist Church in New York City, and received the assurance of her salvation. She testified, *"My very soul was flooded with celestial light. For the first time I realized that I had been trying to hold the world in one hand and the Lord in the other. Jesus set me free."*

In 51 years she wrote over 8,000 hymns. Our hymn books are

full of them. *"Blessed Assurance," "To God Be the Glory," "Redeemed," "Near the Cross,"* and on and on. Fanny never attempted to write a hymn without first kneeling in prayer. She was often under pressure to meet deadlines. In 1869 she tried to write the words for a tune by composer W. H. Doane. He needed it for a meeting, but the words just wouldn't come. Then she remembered that she had forgotten to pray. Immediately she fell to her knees.

After asking God for His forgiveness and help, the words began to flow, as fast as her assistant could write them down. Words for the beautiful hymn, *"Jesus, Keep Me Near the Cross,"* came forth to bless generations to come.

One day in 1874, Fanny Crosby, who received an average of one dollar for each of her hymns, had run short of money. She needed five dollars, even change. She simply prayed. Her prayer ended; she was walking to and fro in her room, trying to get in the mood for another hymn. A man, who was a great admirer of hers, knocked on the door.

She greeted the stranger with her usual *"God bless your dear soul"*. They chatted briefly. In the parting handshake, the man left something in Fanny's hand. It was a five dollar bill. Again going to her knees—now in thanks—she rose from her knees to write, *"All the Way My Savior Leads Me."*

One of Fanny Crosby's hymns was so personal, that for years, she would not let others see it. One day, at a Bible Conference, Evangelist, Dwight L. Moody, asked her to give her personal testimony.

At first, she hesitated. Then she quietly rose to her feet and said, *"There is one hymn I have written, which has never been published. I call it my soul's poem. Sometimes when I am troubled, I recite it, for it brings comfort to my heart."*

Tears began to flow throughout that great company gathered that day, as Fanny Crosby, with blinded eyes, recited the hymn that meant so much to her: *"SAVED BY GRACE"*

"Some day the silver cord will break, And I no more as now

shall sing; But O, the joy when I shall wake Within the palace of the King!

"And I shall see Him face to face, And tell the story, Saved by grace; And I shall see him face to face, And tell the story, Saved by grace."

"I believe myself still really in the prime of life!" wrote Fanny Crosby at the age of 83. She lived 12 more years, and when she died on February 12, 1915, at 95 years of age, the news flashed around the world that America's beloved composer of gospel songs, had gone home to be with her Lord and at last could see face to face the Savior she loved so much. *She was truly free.*

CHAPTER 19

ABRAHAM LINCOLN

FROM LOG CABIN TO A MANSION

One day in 1809 at Hodgenville, Kentucky, two men met. They hailed from the same town, but one had been away from home for a while. *"Any news down at the village, Ezra?"* the latter inquired.

"Nothing at all," came the reply, *"nothing at all, except that a baby has been born at Tom Lincoln's house. Nothing ever happens out here."*

Yet, that birth was one of the greatest happenings in American history. The baby was Abraham Lincoln. George Washington is called the *father* of the nation...Abraham Lincoln, the *savior* of the nation, and the *great emancipator.*

Never before in the nation's history had there been so unusual a time! A man had been elected president, though not even appearing on the ballot in ten states! Even before arriving in Washington, every mail delivery brought more death threats and ominous warnings.

Close friends advised that he resign before taking the oath of office! A plot to assassinate the president elect had been uncovered forcing the last leg of his trip to Wahington to be in the dead of night, without family, under heavy guard, and incognito!

Never before had a President elect faced so unusual a task! Six states had *already* seceded from the Union before the inauguration! A secessionist government had been established. Large quantities of munitions were on their way to Confederate forts, and a siege on the City of Washington had been plotted! Disunity reigned...hatred and distrust abounded...the North *against* the South, friend against friend, and brother against brother!

But, never before had so unusual a man been elected President of the United States! One day as he stood looking at himself in the mirror, a *tall, gaunt, strange-looking man, with arms and legs totally out of proportion to his torso, shrivelled skin, and ears that seemed to flap in the wind,* he exclaimed, *"It's true, Abe Lincoln, you are the ugliest man in the world. If I ever see a man uglier than you, I'm going to shoot him on the spot!"*

A trek to greatness from the depths of insignificance, and the overcoming of tremendous obstacles along the way to success, is a familiar tale in America. But one would be hard-pressed to discover a rise to greatness from a more wretched origin than the life of Abe Lincoln.

The dirt-floor, one-room log cabin that he was born in, well depicts the stark poverty and sheer difficulty of life that surrounded Lincoln as a boy. Lincoln once said, *"God must have loved the common man; He made so many of them."*

And yet, he was blessed and enriched by a religious heritage that would shape his life and prepare him for one of the most monumental tasks of all history.

His mother, Nancy Lincoln, created a religious atmosphere in that cabin home, and spent Sunday afternoons often, with Abe upon her knee, reading to him from the family Bible, and especially impressing upon him the Ten Commandments.

Her last words to him when he was but nine years of age were, *"Abe, I'm going to leave you now and I shall not return. Love your heavenly Father and keep His commandments."* She made him promise never to smoke or drink. He kept that promise.

Sarah Bush, who became Abe's stepmother, reinforced the religious impact of his mother. She took Abe and his sister, Sarah, to the Pigeon Creek Baptist Church every Sunday.

Having learned to read and write in a one room school, a nine-mile walk from home, he began, eagerly, to devour every printed page that fell into his hand. He read and reread, *Robinson Crusoe, Pilgrim's Progress,* and the *King James Bible.*

During the dark days of the Civil War, Lincoln declared a National Day of Prayer and Fasting. He wrote: *"It is the duty of nations as well as of men to own their dependence upon the overruling power of God; to confess their sins and transgressions in humble sorrow... and to recognize the sublime truth announced in the Holy Scriptures and proven by all history that those nations only are blessed whose God is the Lord."*

"Fourscore and seven years ago...". These words began one of the most famous speeches in American history—Abraham Lincoln's *"Gettysburg Address."*

On Nov. 19, 1863, Lincoln dedicated the national cemetery at Gettysburg, Pennsylvania, where a few months earlier 51,000 men were *killed, wounded* or *captured* in one of the bloodiest battles of the Civil War.

Despite the fact that he was the President of the United States, Lincoln was not the event's featured speaker. That honor went to Edward Everett, the former governor of Massachusetts, who was famous for his oratory.

Approximately 60,000 people gathered for the dedication ceremony, and local townspeople sold refreshments and souvenirs, including minie balls and buttons retrieved from the battlefield. *Everett's speech lasted three minutes shy of two hours,* and while he spoke, Lincoln made last-minute changes to his remarks.

When Lincoln finished his *269-word address,* he was not happy with his performance. According to historians, he told a friend, *"It's a flat failure."* Some newspaper accounts agreed.

But history has proclaimed it one of the greatest speeches ever given. *"Fourscore and seven years ago, our fathers brought forth on this continent a new nation, conceived in liberty and dedicated to the proposition that all men are created equal...we here highly resolve that these dead shall not have died in vain; that this nation, under God, shall have a new birth of freedom, and that government of the people, by the people, for the people, shall not perish from the earth."*

When the tragedy of the sudden death of his youngest son, little Willie, the apple of the president's eye, struck the White House, Willie's nurse *shared* with the president her very real and personal relationship with Christ. Lincoln, by his own testimony, did not immediately respond, but some time later he related to a friend, "*When I left Springfield, I asked the people to pray for me; I was not a Christian. When I buried my son—the severest trial of my life—I was not a Christian. But when I went to Gettysburg, and saw the graves of thousands of our soldiers, I then and there consecrated myself to Christ.*" With deep emotion he told his friends that he had at last found the peace for which he longed.

Palm Sunday, 1865 was marked by rejoicing in the city streets of the North. General Robert E. Lee had surrendered at Appomattox.

Five days later, on Good Friday, church bells began to peal in Washington, then in Philadelphia, then in New York City and across the nation; *the president was dead by an assassin's bullet.*

Like his *Savior,* Abe Lincoln. died on Good Friday. He, who saved a nation and set an enslaved people *free,* was now with his *Savior* and *free* from this *vail* of *tears.* He who was born in a log cabin, was *now living* in a mansion, in a city, whose streets are *paved* with gold.

"*Let not your heart be troubled, ye believe in God, believe also in me. In my Father's house are many mansions: if it were not so, I would have told you. I go to prepare a place for you. And if I go and prepare a place for you, I will come again and receive you unto myself; that where I am, there ye may be also.*" (John 14:1-3)

CHAPTER 20

HOW THE WEST WAS WON

At the time of the American Revolution, all West of the Appalachian Mountains was considered untamed wilderness. Even Kentucky and Tennessee were considered a wilderness. Daniel Boon and other adventurous souls ventured into these areas to explore, and opened up the way for settlers to follow.

Then in 1803, President Thomas Jefferson purchased from France, the city of New Orleans, and all the territory West of the Mississippi River, as far as the Rocky Mountains. It was known as the *"Louisiana Purchase"* and was a tremendous bargain, just $15,000,000. Hardly pocket money for the politicians, today.

Then in 1804, an exploring expedition was launched by Meriwether Lewis, (*private secretary of President Jefferson*) and Captain William Clark. They explored the length of the Missouri River as far as the Columbia River. It opened up the Oregon territory and led eventually to the famous Oregon Trail, traveled by so many as they headed West.

Settlers, also moved into Texas, still claimed by Mexico. It resulted in the famous battle of the *"Alamo"* in San Antonio. Colonel William Travis was in charge. He faced the embattled defenders: *"Men, the Mexican dictator, General Santa Ana, has demanded our surrender. But this fort is essential to the defense of Texas. My orders are to hold it. There is no help coming to reinforce us. The Mexicans are about 5,000 strong."*

Then as the 232 American soldiers watched, Colonel Travis drew a line on the dirt floor with his sword. *"Any man who wants to escape is free to go now; any who are determined to stay and die in defense of the Alamo will cross this line."*

Strong-muscled, Davy Crockett, boldly stepped across. Others followed, and finally only James Bowie (*who made the Bowie knife famous*) was left, too ill to move by his own strength. He asked to be carried across.

Colonel Travis sent the fateful message: *"We refuse to surrender."*

The Mexicans attacked on March 6, 1838. It took three assaults for them to overpower the fort by sheer mass of numbers. The Americans fought back grimly, fiercely, but inevitably all lay dead.

When news of their bravery leaked to American forces, the defenders were inspired to advance. General Sam Houston gave the battle cry: *"Victory is certain! Remember the Alamo."* The motto fired the men on to victory over the Mexican army and the dictator, Santa Ana.

In early 1860 the following ad appeared in newspapers across the country.

> "WANTED—*Young, skinny, wiry fellows not over 18.*
> *Must be expert riders willing to risk death daily.*
> *Orphans preferred."*

Hundreds of boys answered the help-wanted ad to become riders for the PONY EXPRESS.

A dozen years earlier, a California ranch foreman had seen a speck of gold shining in a river bed near Sutter's Mill. That first tiny speck of gold started a human stampede, called the Great California Gold Rush. By 1860 gold fever had brought nearly one-half million people from the East to California.

They hungered for mail from their families and friends. But it took months for letters to cross the country. The fastest way at the time to move mail west, was on the famous *"Butterfield Stage"*. It was a 2,800 mile route from Missouri, by way of El Paso, San Diego and finally San Francisco, taking a month or more.

William Hepburn Russell believed he knew a faster way. With good old American ingenuity and enterprise he mapped out a trail from Missouri to Sacramento, through 1,800 miles of western wilderness. Over that trail he built 190 stations. Next he bought horses, wild mustangs, 500 in all. Finally, eighty young men were selected to race the mail across the continent in relays. It would take only 10 days to get the mail through.

Russell was a deeply religious man. He gave each of the boys an engraved Bible and made them swear, *"I will, under no circumstances, use profane language; I will drink no intoxicating liquors; I will not quarrel or fight with any other employees of the firm..."*

On the afternoon of April 3, 1860, hundreds of people gathered in St. Joseph, Mo. A band played stirring music. The crowd cheered. And the first pony rider galloped out of town, carrying a mail pouch destined for California. At about the same time, another pony rider rode out of Sacramento, headed east.

The boy heroes of the Pony Express carried their mail over mountains and deserts, through mud, rain, sleet, and blizzards—and through the heart of hostile Indian country.

Relay stations were spaced five to ten miles apart to provide fresh horses. The rider was allowed just two minutes to leap off his old horse and jump onto the fresh one and thunder away in a cloud of dust. Swing or home stations were spaced between 50 and 100 miles apart. There the rider ate and slept between runs.

A number of very famous people got their start with the Pony Express. Among these were *"Buffalo Bill"* Cody, who was a rider at 15, and *"Wild Bill"* Hickok, who was a station-keeper.

It is said that the Pony Express gave birth to the doughnut. Johnny Frey liked to eat sweet biscuits while racing his horse over his run. But Frey was so dedicated to speeding his mail from station to station that he could never spare the time to stop and pick up a biscuit at his girl friend's house. So his girl friend baked a biscuit with a hole in the middle. Then she stood on the side of the trail holding it out. Johnny Frey rode by, speared the biscuit with his finger, and carried it away without a pause.

The history of the Pony Express was glamorous but short. The service lasted only a year and a half. In that time it achieved all its goals save one. It never made a profit for its owners. In fact, Mr. Russell lost $200,000 on the venture. The last blow came with the completion of the transcontinental telegraph constructed along the same route as the Pony Express. On October 26, 1861, newspapers reported: *"The Pony Express Will Be Discontinued From This Date."*

During its short life the Pony Express delivered more than 30,000 pieces of mail. Remarkably, only one mail pouch was ever lost. To conserve weight, clothing was very light, saddles were extremely small and thin, and no weapons were carried. The horses themselves wore small shoes or none at all. The mail pouches were flat and vary small in size. Letters had to be written on thin paper, and postage was $5.00 an ounce (*a tremendous sum in those days*). Yet, each rider carried a full-sized BIBLE!

In the Black Hills of South Dakota, stands a memorial to four of America's great Presidents. Washington, Jefferson, Lincoln and Theodore Roosevelt. Each is remembered by a likeness, 60 feet high, carved out of the granite face of Mount Rushmore. The heads are in the proportion of men 465 feet tall.

The faces are said to look down on the ages ahead with the wisdom of the past. Most have heard a great deal about Washington, Jefferson and Lincoln, but some ask why *"Teddy"* Roosevelt is among them. Although he is remembered, especially for his use of the word *"bully"* as an adjective, and the words, *"Speak softly and carry a big stick,"* he left his mark on the pages of American history as one of the most forthright and corageous Presidents we have had.

In 1884, Roosevelt's first wife, Alice, and his mother died within a few hours of each other. Overwhelmed with the sorrow and loneliness, he left New York for the Badlands of Dakota Territory. There in the next two years he mastered his sorrow as he lived in the saddle—driving cattle, hunting, and capturing three thieves.

In all his adventures, both in his youth and as a man, he showed utter fearlessness.

"Teddy" carried two pairs of glasses—one for close-up work and the other for seeing things at a distance. While speaking in the city of Milwaukee during his last political campaign, he was shot by a man named Shrenk. He was hurt but insisted on finishing his speech.

Later, when a surgeon was examining his wound, he discovered the steel spectacle case in his vest pocket had saved his life, for it had deflected the bullet from his heart. *"That's remarkable"* said the President, *"I've always considered it a nuisance to carry two pairs of glasses, yet tonight, God used it to save my life."*

Roosevelt became a military hero of the Spanish-American War. As a lieutenant colonel, he led his *"Rough Riders"* up San Juan Hill, freeing Cuba from the rule of Spain, and moving America away from it's former isolationism to become an international power.

At the death of President William McKinley by assassination, Vice President Roosevelt at 42 became the nation's youngest President. During his presidency (1901-1909), the Panama Canal was begun, Orville and Wilbur Wright made their first flight, and the Ford Motor Co. introduced the Model T (and mass production). An earthquake devastated San Francisco.

In the spring of 1903, Roosevelt toured the West, noting in many places how the uncontrolled exploitation of lands, forests, mineral, and water was threatening our natural resources. He camped in Yosemite Park with naturalist, John Muir, and became converted to Muir's view that it could best be preserved under Federal control. It was the beginning of our National Park system.

President Theodore Roosevelt was a man of deep religious faith. He considered church attendance so important that he attended every Sunday, rain or shine. If for some reason he could not attend, he would phone or write a letter to his pastor, explaining his absence.

He was a great supporter of Christian missions. He said, *"Since becoming President, I have come to know that the finest of Americans* we have abroad today are the missionaries of the Cross. I am humiliated that I am not finding out until this late day the worth of foreign missions and the nobility of the missionaries. Their courage is thrilling and their fortitude heroic."

Having experienced first hand the *"Wild, Wild, West"*, Roosevelt had some new coins minted with the words, *"In God We Trust"* removed. *Why?* He didn't think it was *"fitten"* for God's name to be on the coins used in the Brothels, Saloons, and Gambling Halls, so prevalent in the West. He was accused of being an atheist; (*the people just didn't understand his motives*). *"In God We Trust"* was immediately restored to America's Currency.

Next time you hug your *"Teddy Bear"* remember it was named after *"Teddy"* Roosevelt, whose face is carved on Mount Rushmore. Although born in the East, one of his greatest achievements as President was the *"Winning of the West."*

Industrialist/inventor, R. G. LeTourneau, became one of the world's most prosperous of business men. Look across the job site of almost any construction project and if you see a monstrous piece of machinery, one that does the work of a hundred men or more, or one that combines seven operations into one, chances are R. G. LeTourneau had something to do with its invention or original design. Without the machines that LeTourneau dreamed of, conceived, designed, and built, the technological age we now live in might never have happened. We might still be driving on twisting, two-lane roads across the country instead of on sprawling super highways.

"I was raised in a Christian home by a father and mother who loved Jesus and served Him with all their hearts", LeTourneau relates. *"We had a family altar where we worshiped God. Father prayed and asked God to make his children useful in His kingdom. In spite of that, at the age of sixteen I found myself on the wrong road going the wrong way. I began to realize that something was wrong in my life. I tried to turn over a new leaf many times, but each time I failed and each time I got worse."*

It was not until he returned home on the final night of a Revival meeting that he found what he had been searching for. Unable to sleep as he considered his accountability before God, he cried out in desperation, *"Lord, save me or I perish!"* God at that moment became real to him and he knew without a doubt he possessed the full reality of salvation in Christ. LeTourneau's new relationship with Christ made an immediate difference in the way in which he approached life's challenges. Rather than complain, he began to look for divine purpose in each suffering or set-back—and there were plenty.

Shortly after his conversion, the foundry where he worked, burned to the ground, throwing him out of work. He moved to San Francisco to seek work there, only to find himself awakened in the middle of a devastating earthquake. Though at first he thought it was judgment day, he survived by leaving his second-floor apartment as it reached ground level!

He opened an auto-repair shop and dealership in Stockton, where he suffered a broken neck in a stock-car crash and barely survived a gasoline-doused flash fire in the shop. He nearly died of influenza, lost his firstborn son at less than four months of age, and was then plunged into bankruptcy by an inept business partner.

In LeTourneau's own account of that time in his life, he recalls: *"I reviewed my past, and saw where I had been paying only token tribute to God, going through the motions of acting like a Christian, but really serving myself instead of serving God. Like so many, he had accepted Christ as his Savior, but not the Lord of his life."*

He summed it up this way: *"I think the secret of a real out-and-out Christian life is to fall in love with the Lord...If you're not serving the Lord, it proves you don't love Him; if you don't love Him, it proves you don't really know Him. Because to know Him is to love Him, and to love Him is to serve Him."* He determined to *"Seek first the kingdom of God and His righteousness." (Matt. 6:33)* trusting that God would take care of the rest.

Though their difficulties did not disappear overnight ,and the pain of losing their firstborn was with them for a lifetime; spiritually, Bob and Evelyn LeTourneau were never the same. Within a short period of time they were deeply involved in the evangelistic efforts of the Christian and Missionary Alliance Church.

He told Forbes magazine, *"I like to do two things. One is to design machines, turn on the power, and see them work. The other is to turn on the power of the Gospel and see it work in people's lives."*

He did pretty well in the first department. At his death in 1969 he held over 200 patents. One of his monster earth-moving machines, weighing 200,000 pounds, can cut a thirty-five-foot swath through a jungle, knocking down trees five feet in diameter and chewing them up.

He did well in the second department, too. Besides giving up to ninety percent of his income which was many millions of dollars, to Christian work, he would fly anywhere to speak for Jesus Christ. He is the only man to have been president of both the Christian Businessmen's Committee, International and Gideons, International.

R. G. LeTourneau believed that Jesus meant it when he said: *"Lay not up for yourselves treasures upon earth, where moth and rust doth corrupt, and where thieves break through and steal: But lay up for yourselves treasures in heaven, where neither moth nor rust doth corrupt and where thieves do not break through nor steal: For where your treasure is there will your heart be also."* (Matt. 6:19-21) He often said: *"It is not how much money I give to God, but how much of God's money I keep for myself."*

CHAPTER 21

SALVATION ARMY,

GOD'S GOOD SAMARITANS

On April 10, 1829 was born in Nottingham, England, a man whose love for Christ would raise the social conscience of the world in behalf of the poor, the needy, and the outcasts of society. That man was William Booth, founder of the Salvation Army.

William Booth was born in poverty, himself, and at the age of 13 was apprenticed to a pawnbroker. In 1844, however, something happened that transformed his life, and catapulted him into world history. *He found Christ as his personal Savior.*

From *"The Authoritative Life of General Booth"* by C. S. Railton is his own account of what happened. *"When as a giddy youth of fifteen I was led to attend Wesley Chapel, Nottingham ...I was wrought upon quite independently of human effort by the Holy Ghost, who created within me a great thirst for a new life...One feeling specially forced itself upon me...and that was the sense of the folly of spending my life in doing things for which I knew I must either repent or be punished in the days to come.*

"...I remember, as if it were but yesterday...the instant rolling away from my heart of the guilty burden, the peace that came in its place, and the going forth to serve my God and my generation from that hour...Since that night...when the happy change was realised, the business of my life has been...to live a life of loving activity in the service of God and man."

At seventeen, Booth was made a local preacher in the Methodist church. His superintendent wanted him to become a regular preacher at the age of nineteen. But his doctor advised him against the ministry, telling him that his health was so poor that he was totally unfit for the strain of the preacher's life. He didn't take his doctor's advice and he died in 1912 at 83 years of age!

In 1865 Booth organized the *East London Revival Society* in the Whitechapel district of the London slums and in 1878 it became known as the *Salvation Army*. Preaching in the slums of London, he declared to all that would listen, *"There is a heaven in East London for everyone who will stop and listen and think and look to Christ."* For his efforts he was pelted with garbage and curses.

In pouring rain he fell upon his knees and cried out, *"Lord, what must I do? Is this your will for me? I don't know where to start. Use me for your purpose."* He rose from his knees to raise an army, one by one, to reach out in Christian love to help meet the physical needs of the downtrodden, but most of all to meet their spiritual needs through Christ.

Booth said, *"It is not enough to put a pair of new britches on a man, to give him regular work, or even a University education—all these are outside of man—if the inside remains unchanged, you have wasted your labor."* In fact, he said, *"I consider that the chief dangers which will confront the 20th century will be: Religion without the Holy Spirit, Christianity without Christ, Forgiveness without regeneration, Morality without God, and Heaven without hell."*

March 10, 1880, one man and seven frail women landed unheralded and hardly noticed at Castle Garden, N.Y., carrying their luggage, a tamborine, several brass horns, and a flag, to claim America for God.

When they began to preach the claims of Christ in front of the taverns and brothels of New York, they were not warmly received. Officials of the city ran them out at the insistence of the tavern and brothel owners, who were losing business. The Salvation Army periodical, "War Cry" reported in 1894 that one of *"God's Army"* had been brutally murdered for his preaching in St. Louis. Lynchings, shootings, and other attacks on Salvation Army *"soldiers"* occurred also in San Francisco, Pittsburg, Brooklyn, Los Angeles and other cities across the nation.

But, then, on April 18, 1906 the San Francisco earthquake hit. The Salvation Army pitched in, attending to the needs of the victims for food, clothing and shelter. World War I broke out and in 1917 Evangeline Booth, youngest daughter of William Booth, convinced General Pershing, that the Salvation Army could be of help to the boys in the muddy trenches of France.

As they set sail, Evangeline said, *"We must be an example of Christ's love—lay down our lives if need be—under the banner of Christ by which alone men can be delivered from their bondage of sin."* For her sacrificial service, President Woodrow Wilson awarded Evangeline the *"Distinguished Service Medal"*. In World War II the Salvation Army not only continued their unselfish service, but helped found the U.S.O.

I am told that in any given year, many thousands of alcoholics and drug addicts are reclaimed through the power of Christ and the ministry of the Salvation Army. The homeless are given shelter. Unwed mothers are cared for. Missing persons are traced. The jobless find jobs. Millions of meals are served and as many families given financial aide.

But most of all, millions hear the gospel of Christ proclaimed in Salvation Army Chapels and on street corners around the world. The *"good news"* that *"God so loved the world that He gave His only begotten Son, that whosoever believeth on Him should not perish, but have everlasting life."* (John 3:16) And that, *"The Lord is...not willing that any should perish, but that all should come to repentance."* (2 Peter 3:9)

For many years the Salvation Army and William Booth in particular were subjected to some of the most vile persecution suffered by Christians in modern times. But the General lived to see the day his Army would be honored around the world.

King Edward VII invited him to Buckingham Palace in 1904. The king said, *"You are doing a good work—a great work, General Booth."* He asked him to write in his autograph album. The old man—now 75—bent forward, took the pen, and sumed up his life's work: *"Your Majesty. Some men's ambition is art, Some men's ambition is fame, Some men's ambition is gold, My ambition is the souls of men."*

When the *"Empress of Ireland"* went down with 130 Salvation Army officers on board, 109 officers were drowned, and not one body that was picked up had on a life belt. The few survivors told how the Salvationists, both men and women, finding there were not enough life preservers for all, took off their own belts and strapped them even upon strong men, saying, *"I can die better than you can"*.

They had a peace and an assurance in Christ that nothing could shake. They could say with the Psalmist, *"Yea, though I walk through the valley of the shadow of death, I will fear no evil; for thou art with me..."* (Ps 23:4)

CHAPTER 22

ALCOHOLIC'S ANONYMOUS AND A POWER GREATER THAN THEMSELVES

Alexander the Great was ruler of Macedonia at age 16, victorious general at 18, king at 20—and then died a drunkard before age 33. He had conquered the then-known world, but not himself.

Bemoaning the fact that there were no more worlds to conquer, he held a banquet in the city of Babylon. On the second night of carousal, he drank to the health of every person there. He then called for *"Hercules' cup,"* which had a huge capacity. Filling it, he gulped it all down. He called for it to be refilled. He held it high in a toast to the *"gods,"* and suddenly fell to the floor. In a few days, he was dead.

Telling an alcohol addict to shape up and stop drinking is like telling a man who jumps out of a nine-story building to fall only three floors. Because of the alcoholic's helplessness, and because addiction follows a predictable pattern and has a pronounced inheritance factor, it is not inappropriate to call alcoholism a disease.

"First the man takes a drink, then the drink takes a drink, then the drink takes the man." This ancient proverb says it well. Whatever label we attach to alcoholism, the alcoholic has set in motion powerful forces over which he has no control.

The three leading causes of death in the United States are heart disease, cancer, and alcohol related deaths. Among these three, alcoholism, however, occupies a unique position: It is completely preventable; and it is highly treatable.

The alcoholic does not need condemnation, any more than the heart or cancer victim. Down deep the alcoholic knows he is his own worst enemy and drinks to drown his guilt. Neither does he need an *"enabler"* to help him avoid the consequences of his drinking. But what he does need is *"tough love."*

Bill W. was a New York Stock Broker. Before the great depression, he made money hand over fist. But then suddenly in Oct. 1929 the crash came, and fortunes of millions, including Bill's were destroyed. The papers reported men jumping to their death from the towers of High Finance.

Liquor ceased to be a luxury to Bill; it became a necessity. *"Bathtub"* gin, two bottles a day, and often three, got to be routine. He would waken very early in the morning shaking violently. A tumbler full of gin followed by half a dozen bottles of beer would be required before he could eat breakfast.

This continued for years until he was rushed to the hospital with delirium tremens and probable heart failure. He was developing *"wet brain"* and would either be dead or in the Asylum in a few days. Alcohol was his master. He had lost his livelihood, the respect of his wife and family, his health, and death seemed the only possible solution to his despair.

Then he got a call and visit from an old school chum and drinking buddy. The door opened and his friend stood there with a glow on his face. There was something about his eyes. He was inexplicably different. He said, *"I've got religion."*

In a matter of fact way, he told of having found freedom from his slavery to alcohol by *"faith in God."* He had tried everything and nothing worked. Doctors had pronounced him incurable. He was near death's door when he found the answer. His human will had failed but he found a power beyond himself.

Bill had little use for religion and always thought of those who did, as *"holier than thou"* and *"hypocrites."* He believed that there was a God out there somewhere, but he didn't believe in a personal God that was interested in or related in a personal way to human beings. Surely, if He did, there wouldn't be so much suffering in the world, he thought. But before his eyes stood a miracle.

Bill W. wanted a miracle in his own life. He says, *"I, too, offered myself to God to do with me as He would. I placed myself unreservedly under His care and direction. I admitted for the first time that of myself I was nothing; that without Him I was lost. I ruthlessly, faced my sins and became willing to have my new-found Friend take them away, root and branch..."*

Dr. Bob was a leading surgeon. He grew up in church, but when he went to college and medical school, drinking with his fraternity brothers became a favorite pastime. He managed to get his degree, however, and opened a medical practice. He developed stomach trouble and discovered that a couple of drinks would alleviate his gastric distress, at least for a few hours at a time.

He had two distinct phobias. One was the fear of not sleeping, and the other was the fear of running out of liquor. His phobia about sleeplessness demanded that he get drunk every night, but in order to get more liquor for the next night, he had to stay sober during the day. This routine went on for seventeen years. He would promise his wife, his chidren and friends that he would drink no more—promises which he seldom kept even through the day—even though very sincere when he made them.

Dr. Bob says; *"How my wife kept her faith and courage during all those years, I'll never know, but she did. If she had not, I know I would have been dead a long time ago. For some reason, we alcoholics seem to have the gift of picking out the world's finest women. Why they should be subjected to the tortures we inflict upon them, I cannot explain."*

At his wife's behest, they made friends with a group of people that attracted them because of their seeming poise, health, and happiness. One had been an alcoholic and found deliverance through faith in God. Dr. Bob paid attention to what he had to say because this man had been there—an alcoholic himself—and demonstrated a genuine concern and love.

On June 10, 1935, Dr. Bob took his last drink. He states; *"If you think you are an atheist, an agnostic, skeptic, or have any other form of intellectual pride which keeps you from accepting a power greater than yourself. If you still think you are strong enough to beat the game alone, that is your affair. But if you really and truly want to quit drinking liquor for good and all, we have an answer for you. It never fails, if you go about it with half the zeal you go after drink."* Dr. Bob says, *"Your Heavenly Father will never let you down."*

In 1935, two hard-drinking alcoholics, Bill W. and Dr. Bob, whom doctors had long dismissed as hopeless drunks, organized *"Alcoholics Anonymous"*. The *"Power"* greater than themselves, that gave both Bill W. and Dr. Bob the strength to overcome their addiction was *Christ*.

Today, decades later, *Alcoholics Anonymous* is a vessel of hope for millions of alcoholics throughout the world. It is an organization which is supported only by voluntary contributions from its members and has no rules, no officers, no *"pecking order,"* no publicity drives, no outside contributions, and no form of promotion save its success in bringing sobriety to hopeless drunks.

There are many profit-making and expensive alcoholism treatment programs, but none with the success rate of *Alcoholics Anonymous*. Even most of these recommend that those that have gone through their program join an AA group afterwards.

Members of AA help one another *"grow along spiritual lines"* through weekly meetings; a one-on-one sponsorship program, and by being available around the clock to answer calls for help from recovering alcoholics, who unexpectedly find themselves tempted to drink.

The atmosphere of an AA meeting is a mixture of loving acceptance, laughter, and the most honest communication anywhere. The knowledge that they share with one another about a dangerous addiction creates an openness and bond of fellowship that is seldom found in any other area of society.

The Twelve Step program composed by the founders of Alcoholics Anonymous has proven itself over and over again, not only for recovery from alcohol addiction but almost evey other addiction. Almost every recovering addict has followed the same path.

1. We admitted we were powerless over alcohol—that our lives had become unmanageable.
2. Came to believe that a Power greater than ourselves could restore us to sanity.
3. Made a decision to turn our will and our lives over to the care of God .
4. Made a searching and fearless moral inventory of ourselves.
5. Admitted to God, to ourselves, and to another human being the exact nature of our wrongs.
6. Were entirely ready to have God remove all these defects of character.
7. Humbly asked Him to remove our shortcomings.
8. Made a list of persons we had harmed, and became willing to make amends to them all.
9. Made direct amends to such people wherever possible, except when to do so would injure them or others.
10. Continued to take personal inventory and when we were wrong promptly admitted it.
11. Sought through prayer and meditation to improve our conscious contact with God, praying only for knowledge of His will for us and the power to carry that out.
12. Having had a spiritual awakening as the result of these steps, we tried to carry this message to other alcoholics, and to practice these principles in all our affairs.

Their daily prayer is: *"God, grant me the serenity to accept the things I cannot change; Courage to change the things I can; and Wisdom to know the difference."*

CHAPTER 23

WAR TO END ALL WARS

Prompted by widespread fears that new means of mass destruction might wipe out Western civilization, the Pope of Rome issued a bull forbidding their use by any Christian state against another, whatever the provocation.

The hydrogen bomb? Germ warfare? No. It was in 1139 A.D. and was issued by Pope Innocent II. He was talking about the newly invented *"crossbow"*.

In 1867, at age 34, Alfred Bernard Nobel, was granted a patent for dynamite and over the next 29 years of his life he became fabulously wealthy from the manufacture of explosives. When his brother, George, died, a newspaper made a mistake and printed a story stating that Alfred had died. Reading the story of his own death was a shocking experience for Alfred.

He discovered he was a man held in little esteem by his fellow man. He was thought of as a selfish and money grubbing man who cared little, if anything, for others unless they could be of profit to him in some financial way.

Reading the news story had a profound effect on Alfred. He set about at once to change his image. He saw so much destruction as a result of his invention, that in his will he provided for a trust to establish five prizes in the field of peace, physics, chemistry, physiology or medicine, and literature. It was called the *"Nobel Peace Prize"*.

Dr. Robert Oppenheimer, who supervised the creation of the first atomic bomb, appeared before a Congressional Committee.

They inquired of him if there were any defense against the weapon. *"Certainly"*, he replied. *"And that is—"* Dr. Oppenheimer looked over the hushed, expectant audience and said softly: *"Peace."*

Throughout recorded history, man has yearned for and dreamed of peace. On one of the walls of the United Nations building appears a text lifted from Isaiah 2:4. *"They shall beat their swords into plowshares, and their spears into pruning hooks: nation shall not lift up sword against nation, neither shall they learn war any more."* Unfortunately, the first part of that verse has been deleted. The verse begins: *"And He (the Messiah) shall judge among the nations, and shall rebuke many people."* Interestingly, the inscription on the U. N. wall was donated by the Russian government under Stalin.

Since the beginning of recorded history only eight per cent of the time has the world been entirely at peace. In over 3,100 years only 286 have been warless and 8,000 treaties have been broken.

Eighty years ago, Nov. 11, 1918, peace was declared as the Armistice was signed ending World War I. When the Armistice was signed, the nations of the world were convinced that they had just fought the *"war that would end all wars"*. It was believed that man had finally learned his lesson; that he had now *"evolved"* to the place that he was too smart and too civilized to settle differences through the primitive brutality of war. The *"League of Nations"* like the *"United Nations"* was expected to bring about a *"New World Order"* with no more wars.

But in just a few short years, World War II broke out with the brutal atrocities of Hitler and the holocaust. It all started in one of the most *"civilized"* and scientifically advanced countries in Europe. To be educated in a German University was to be truly educated and be courted by the *"intelligentsia"* of the world. Then came the Korean conflict and Vietnam.

In the eighty years since World War I, for every year of war there has been only two minutes of peace in a war weary world. In America, one out of every eight Americans is a war veteran.

General Omar Bradley of World War II fame said, *"Our knowledge of science has already outstripped our capacity to control it. We have too many men of science and too few men of God. We have grasped the mystery of the atom and rejected the Sermon on the Mount. Man is stumbling blindly through a spiritual darkness while toying with the precarious secrets of life and death. The world has achieved brilliance without wisdom, power without conscience. Ours is a world of nuclear giants and ethical infants."*

Lieutenant Gitz Rice was a member of a famous Canadian regiment which went to France in World War I. The regiment fought in Flanders' Fields and across *"No Man's Land"*. Rice's company carried a strange implement of war—a piano. On that piano in France, Gitz Rice composed the famous song, *"Mademoiselle from Armentieres."*

The afternoon before Christmas Eve it was decided that the piano should be taken up to the front-line trenches. It was hoisted into an army truck and finally deposited at its destination. That night peace settled over *"No Man's Land"*. But the barbed wire remained and a morning attack threatened each side. The hostile troops were so close they could hear the rumble of their enemies voices.

Shortly before the hour of midnight, Rice began playing Christmas carols. First he played *"Silent Night, Holy Night"* followed by *"Hark, the Herald Angels Sing"* and other beloved carols familiar to the Christian world.

The Canadian soldiers sang lustily, then they paused. From across the shallow field they heard the German troops singing with them. It was Christmas Eve! Rice then played an aria from Wagner's *"Tannhauser."* As he began the opening chords, a Canadian soldier mounted the rim of the parapet and sang the words.

"More! More!" shouted the Germans. Then one of their own singers, a rich baritone, repeated the song to Rice's accompaniment, standing as a target for British rifles. But not a shot was fired as together they celebrated the birthday of the *"Prince of Peace "*

One day the *"Prince of Peace"*, born on Christmas Day, will be crowned *"King of Kings"* and then, *"...nation shall not lift up sword against nation, neither shall they learn war any more."* (Isa. 2:4) On that day will be fulfilled the song of the angels to lowly shepherds abiding in the Judean fields: *"Glory to God in the highest, and on earth peace, good will toward men."* (Lk. 2:14)

George Bernard Shaw was a brilliant man, a literary genius and yet he rejected the message of Scripture. He placed his trust in his own system of belief, which was based on human reason. Yet he could not find lasting inner peace, and slowly lost confidence in what he believed.

Shortly before Shaw died in 1950, he wrote, *"The science to which I pinned my faith is bankrupt...It's counsels, which should have established the millennium, have led directly to the suicide of Europe. I believed them once...In their name I helped to destroy the faith of millions..And now they look at me and witness the great tragedy of an atheist who has lost his faith (atheism)".*

A bumper sticker several years ago read: *"Visualize World Peace."* In the 1970s John Lennon sang, *"Give peace a chance."* Another song said, *"Imagine there's no heaven...no hell...no war...And then the World will be as one."* Neither idea worked, but God has a better idea.

A little girl tried to assemble a big jigsaw puzzle of a world map. Each piece of the puzzle was shaped like a country. She studied the picture on the box top, but still couldn't figure out how to get all the pieces in the right place.

Finally, in hopeless frustration, she came to her father for help. Her dad turned the puzzle box over, revealing that it was a two-sided puzzle: the world map on one side and a picture of a man on the other. They turned all the puzzle pieces over and quickly put the pieces together to form the picture of a man. Then they turned the puzzle over again, and the world map was perfectly in order. *"I see now, Daddy!"* the little girl said, *"When you get this one man put together, you are getting the world put together right, too!"*

There can be no true peace, either in the human heart or the world, without the presence of the *"Prince of Peace."*

CHAPTER 24

WHY HITLER STARTED A HOLOCAUST

It was the night of Nov. 9, 1938; called *"Kristallnacht"* because of the sparkling shards of glass from thousands of smashed windows. It was a night of terror that marked the dawn of Hitler's Holocaust against the Jews and all who dared to oppose him.

Alfred Jachmann was an 11-year-old in a small town in northern Poland. *"We were sleeping behind shutters with the windows closed,"* he recalled. *"We were jerked out of our sleep by the crashing glass. We heard the screams, 'The synagogue is burning'. My father screamed, 'the sky's all red!' We hid behind him for three hours, shaking from fear and terror. Uniformed Nazis rushed into our house and arrested my father without saying a word.*

My sister, mother and I had to leave Arnswalde within three days," added 61-year-old Jachman, head of the Jewish home for the elderly in Frankfurt. His mother, father and 13-year-old sister all died in the Auschwitz concentration camp. Jachmann, was also sent to Auschwitz, but later, managed to save himself, by plunging into the snow, when Nazi machine-gunners mowed down prisoners in January 1945.

In seven years, Hitler and the Nazis (*National Socialist Party*) ruthlessly tortured and murdered six million Jews and nine million others, who did not fit into his idea of a *"Master Race"*. It was his *"Final Solution"*.

Americans and the rest of the civilized world heard reports of what was going on but refused to believe that such a diabolically monstrous thing could possibly be happening. Surely civilized man had *"evolved"* beyond such cruelty. It was not until I saw it with my own eyes, as part of General Patton's troops that liberated Munich, and the infamous concentration camp of Dachau, and later serving in the Military Government De-Nazification program, that I could believe it. . .

September 1, 1939, World War II began. The German Wehrmacht with one and one-half million troops, with tanks and the Luftwafe, *"blitzkrieged"* across the frontiers of Poland and subjugated its people in just 18 days. In just a few years, Hitler's forces controlled most of Europe and North Africa. During twelve terrible years, 1933-45, one man, Adolph Hitler, gained enormous, almost unbelievable power, and threatened to conquer the world. World War II involved five continents and the death of 50 million people. Two-thirds were civilians.

Hitler was an obscure nobody until the early 1920s. Then, as a political spellbinder, he clawed and climbed his way to sole leadership of the National Socialist Workers Party of Germany. By 1933 he had bargained his way into that nation's top governmental position. As German Chancellor and *"Fuehrer"*, Hitler used terror, threats, and fraud, (*the Big Lie*) to extend his control.

Adolf Hitler was born, April 20, 1889, at Braunau am Inn, Austria. He was the fourth child of Klara Polzl and Alois Schicklgruber. At age 40 Adolph's father changed his name to Hitler, after discovering that his father's name was Hiedler. He seems to have hoped to inherit some money from his supposed uncle, Johann Nepomuck Hiedler.

Adolph's mother, Klara, had been Alois' maid while Alois' second wife was still alive. Alois was a tyrannical father and was constantly berating Adolph about his grades in school. His teachers' comments suggest that he was not stupid, but was very lazy and a difficult personality. He never completed work at any school. In fact, he showed such hatred of school, he once used a report card for toilet paper.

Considering himself an artist, Hitler went to Vienna in hopes of enrolling in the Academy of Fine Arts, but he was turned down. He blamed the rejection on the Jews.

Hitler became interested in the occult and the Ostara movement of Adolf Lanz. Lanz's publications were a mishmash of occultism, astrology, racism, and anti- Semitism. He depicted the world as a great evolutionary struggle between blond supermen and beast-like, racially inferior people. The Ostara movement displayed the *"swastika"* as a symbol as early as 1907.

Hitler's favorite philosopher was Friedrich Nietziche, who went insane in 1889 and died a suicide. Like Marx, he believed that God had to be pushed aside in order for man to be free to be his own god. Therefore, God <u>must</u> not and <u>ought</u> not exist.

To such thinkers as Nietzsche, the traditional moral attributes of God (*e.g. kindness, mercy and love*) were the source of all decadent *"slave ethics."* He turned ethics upside down by calling greed and violence, *"good"* and kindness and mercy, *"evil."* Like most of the evolutionists of that day, he taught that the black race was inferior and was the link between the white race and the apes.

How could such a horrible thing happen? How is it possible that a leader such as Hitler could sway thousands and even millions of intelligent Germans to his cause? It is one thing to say that Hitler was crazy; it is quite something else to affirm that all Germans were crazy along with him. To Hitler, it was but the logical conclusion and outgrowth of his fanatical belief in the basic tenet of evolution, *"survival of the fittest."*

In *"Evolution and Ethics"*, evolutionist, Sir Arthur Keith, states, *"The German Fuhrer... consciously sought to make the practice of Germany conform to the theory of evolution."* In *"Mein Kampf"*, he spoke of *"lower human types."* He criticized the Jews for bringing *"Negroes in the Rhineland"* with the aim of *"ruining the white race..."* He said, *"The stronger must dominate and not blend with the weaker.. Those who want to live, let them fight, and those who do not want to fight in this world of eternal struggle (evolution) do not deserve to live."*

After all, had not Darwin said, *"At some future period, not very distant as measured by centuries, the civilized races of man will almost certainly exterminate, and replace, the savage races throughout the world."* School children in Germany, being force fed evolution, as if it were a proven scientific fact, found it easy to accept Hitler's *"final solution".*

The true Christian does not have the option of racism. Jesus told His followers to *love* their enemies—*not to kill them.* He healed the sick and deformed and showed compassion for the weak and enfeebled.

Lutheran pastor, Martin Neimoller had been a U boat captain in W W I, and was fiercely patriotic. But because of his faith in Christ, could not stomach what Hitler was doing. He became the symbolic figure of the Protestant opposition to Hitler.

The New York Times reported the death of Victor Kugler in 1981 and credited him as the one who *"hid Anne Frank".* The article describes him as a Christian and says that *"he sheltered victims escaping from the Nazi hell at a time when the whole world had closed its doors."*

Corrie ten Boom and her family were sent to the concentration camp at Ravensbruck because they, too, provided a *"hiding place"* for Jews, from Nazi persecution. Corrie was a dedicated Christian.

Rose Warmer was given permission to distribute New Testaments in Israeli public schools (*not allowed in America's schools*) because she as a Christian *"voluntarily went to the infamous Auschwitz death camp with her Jewish friends, during World War II"*

Albert Einstein, the great Jewish physicist, was exiled by Hitler. He said, *"Being a lover of freedom, when the Nazi revolution came, I looked to the universities to defend it, knowing that they had always boasted of their devotion to the cause of truth; but no, the universities were silenced. Then I looked to the newspapers, whose flaming editorials in days gone by, had proclaimed their love of freedom; but they were silenced.*

"Only the Church stood squarely across the path of Hitler's suppressing of truth...the Church alone had the courage and persistence to stand for intellectual and moral freedom. I am forced to confess that what I once despised, I now praise unreservedly."

CHAPTER 25

PEARL HARBOR, THE ATOM BOMB AND WORLD WAR II

It was during the 1930s in the height of the *"Great Depression"* in St. Louis, Mo. As a teenager, I had not the slightest inkling of the part the man who lived just two houses down the street from us would play in world history.

I played *"step ball"* with his son. He had been a pilot and flight instructor in World War I, but in 1930, at age 33, he resigned from the service because of *"advanced age"*. For the next 10 years he worked for the Shell Oil Company in aeronautical research and as a test pilot. I thought he had a strange name. It was *"Jimmy Doolittle"*.

Then came *"Pearl Harbor"*. It was a quiet and peaceful Sunday morning in Hawaii. A time to catch a few extra minutes of sleep. But then, suddenly, without warning at 7:55 a.m., Dec. 7, 1941, all hell broke loose. The Japanese were bombing Pearl Harbor. In just a couple of hours, hundreds of Japanese war planes rained almost total destruction upon America's entire Pacific Fleet. Six major airfields along with almost every plane were destroyed and 2,400 American servicemen killed.

That morning at 7 a.m., while the Japanese warplanes were 137 miles (*50 minutes*) away, two U.S. soldiers on a small radar station in the Pacific scanned the screen and saw a few dots and then more dots appearing, until the whole screen was filled. The soldiers notified their supervisor, a young lieutenant. No other officer was around, since it was Sunday.

The lieutenant thought, surely the dots must be planes from California or American carriers at sea, and without another thought, uttered the fateful words: *"Don't worry about it."* There would have been time to scramble the planes at Pearl Harbor, prepare the battleships and shelter the men. The words, *"Don't worry about it"* changed the course of history.

Hitler with one of the most powerful military machines in history was *"blitzkrieging"* his way across Europe. Country after country had fallen and the holocaust of genocide and concentration camps was *"evolving"* into Hitler's dream of a *"master race"*.

On Dec. 8, President Roosevelt addressed a joint session of Congress, describing the attack as *"a day which will live in infamy..."* America was at war. And Americans were united, as never before, behind the war effort. Almost without exception, every American, with patriotic fervor, made the sacrifices needed to win.

An example of such sacrifice was that of four Chaplains; a Jewish rabbi, a Catholic priest, and two Protestant ministers. They were with the troops on a U. S. transport, the Dorchester, off the coast of Greenland. The ship was torpedoed and began to sink. There were not enough life belts for all the soldiers.

The four chaplains took off their life preservers and handed them to four unequipped soldiers. Minutes later the survivors saw the chaplains going down into the icy waters with the ship, their arms linked, and their voices raised in prayer.

Taken by surprise and ill-prepared, the war in the Pacific did not go well for the U.S. in the following months. The Japanese scored victory after victory with thousands of American citizens taken prisoner or killed.

But then, April 18, 1942, sixteen B-25 bombers under the command of Col. James Doolittle, were launched from the carrier, Hornet. Their mission—to bomb Tokyo. Tokyo was 700 miles away and it was impossible for the planes to return to the carrier after dropping their bombs, so they hoped to reach friendly territory on the Asiatic mainland. Of the 80 heroic men on that almost suicidal mission, most eventually returned to the U.S. via China after their 30 seconds over Tokyo. But eight were captured by the Japanese.

The war raged on. It is June 6, 1944. *"D-Day"* is about to dawn. Tons of equipment and vast numbers of Allied troops have been gathered in southern England, turning the area into a huge military camp.

"Operation Overlord" was under the command of Supreme Allied Commander General Dwight D. Eisenhower. The invasion was originally scheduled for June 5, but the weather did not cooperate.

Eisenhower writes in his book, *"Crusade In Europe"*, *"At three-thirty that morning we were shaking and shuddering under a wind of almost hurricane proportions and the accompanying rain seemed to be traveling in horizontal streaks."* He knew that they could not postpone the invasion more than a few days and still maintain the element of surprise.

Meterologists predicted continued stormy weather for an indefinite period. It began to look like all the preparation and build-up might be for nothing. It was rumored that the Germans had a new secret weapon and were close to developing the atom bomb. A decision had to be made, and Eisenhower had to make it.

Throughout America and England, people were praying. *"Ike"*, too, was a praying man. He said, *"Prayer gives you courage to make the decisions you must make in crisis and then the confidence to leave the result to a Higher Power."* He made the decision.

Eisenhower's Order of the Day to the assault troops as they headed out was: *"The hopes and prayers of liberty-loving people everywhere march with you...let us all beseech the blessing of Almighty God upon this great and noble undertaking."*

Suddenly, just before dawn on that fateful day, the storm ceased and there was unexpected calm. Because of the bad weather, the Germans were convinced there would be no invasion at that time. They were caught totally off guard. German submarines had in one year sunk seven million tons of Allied shipping, but there was not one U-Boat in the Channel that morning to challenge the crossing.

The *London Daily Telegraph* reported: *"It was only that night the U-Boats did not patrol the channel. The way we went over to Normandy was beyond imagination—4,000 ships and 11,000 planes—and they never met a single ship or plane of the enemy!"*

At dawn the main invasion force began to land on a 60-mile stretch of the Normandy coast. Before the day was out, Allied troops, against overwhelming odds and a ceaseless barrage of enemy fire, had secured the beaches. God had answered prayer.

Eisenhower once said, *"It takes no brains to be an atheist. Any stupid person can deny the existence of a supernatural power because man's physical senses cannot detect it. But there cannot be ignored the mystery of first life...or the marvelous order in which the universe moves about us. All of these evidence the handiwork of a beneficent Deity. For my part, that Deity is the God of the Bible and Christ, His Son."*

Billy Graham relates a profoundly moving incident which occurred just before the death of Eisenhower. *"I was invited to go and see him at the Walter Reed Hospital,"* the evangelist records. *"I went in. He had his normal big smile. He knew he did not have long to live. I was told I could stay thirty minutes. But when the thirty minutes were up, Ike wanted me to stay longer. He said: 'Billy, tell me once again how I can be sure my sins are forgiven, and that I am going to Heaven, because nothing else matters now.'"*

Billy took out his New Testament and read from 1 John 5:11-13, *"And this is the testimony that God has given us eternal life and this life is in His Son. He who has the Son has life; he who does not have the Son of God does not have life. These things I have written to you who believe in the name of the Son of God, that you may know that you have eternal life..."*

Billy explained, *"We go to Heaven not because of our good works, or because of money we may have given to the church. We go to heaven totally and completely on the basis of the merits of what Christ did on the cross. We can be sure of our salvation because Jesus paid it all!"*

"For by grace are ye saved, through faith, and that not of our selves,

it is the gift of God, not of works, lest any man should boast." (Eph. 2:8-9).

"Ike" looked at Billy and said, *"I'm ready."* They prayed, and as Billy turned to leave, he asked him if he was going to Vietnam. When Billy assured him that he was, *"Ike"* said, *"Tell them an old "doughboy" is praying for them."*

Quietly, peacefully, Dwight David Eisenhower, Supreme Commander of Allied Forces, World War II, loved as a friend to us GIs, President of Columbia University, a national hero, elected President of the United States by an unprecedented popular vote, twice, slipped into the presence of the Savior he loved and trusted for his eternal salvation.

August 5, 1945, at 8:15 a.m., the city of Hiroshima, Japan, awoke after a restless night of alarms. At that moment a bomb, nicknamed *"Fat Boy"*, detached itself from the B-29 *"Enola Gay"*. Forty-three seconds later a purple flash dazzled the city.

A huge ball of fire engulfed the center and waves of heat, three times the temperature of the sun, rolled across the city, with shock waves from the explosion equal to that of 20,000 tons of TNT. Then the *"atomic mushroom"* rose up miles above the city, which had almost instantaneously become a desert.

Fire engulfed the city, the wind raged and the *"black rain"* began to fall. The survivors were soon shaking with cold. Eighty thousand people were killed and thousands more injured. Three days later another bomb was dropped on Nagasaki. *On August 14 Japan surrendered.*

With Hitler a suicide and Germany defeated and in ruins, many of us GIs in the European theatre had been anticipating the likelihood of being shipped out to the other side of the world to join the GIs in the Pacific. Until that day when Japan surrendered, most believed that an invasion of the Japanese mainland was the only way to bring an end to the war. It was estimated that a million or more would die as a result and there would be years more of war.

As horrible as was the devastation wrought on that day, almost without exception, Americans applauded the courageous decision of President Truman to drop the bomb.

Japan surrendered and we, who had enlisted for the duration, rejoiced to know that we would soon be going home to good old "Uncle Sugar" and those we loved.

At that time America, with the atomic bomb, was the most powerful nation on earth and could have conquered the world. Atheistic Russia under Stalin subjugated and plundered every nation it's armies set foot upon and then set out by subversion to conquer the world with communism.

Americans, instead, taxed themselves and through the Marshall plan sent billions of dollars to their former enemies to feed their people and rebuild their cities and economies, so that they could be free. It was the expected thing for Americans to do, for the traditional values of America came from the Bible and the teachings of Christ. Had not Jesus said, *"Love your enemies,..."* (Matt. 5:44)

Some ten years after the dropping of the bomb, I was at a Baptist Pastors' Conference in Los Angeles. The speaker was Mitsuo Fuchida. Commander Fuchida had led the attack by the Japanese on Pearl Harbor.

We listened intently as Fuchida spoke to us in halting English. He said, *"I believed that the gods had laid their hands on me and protected my life for some strange reason, but I didn't know why. At that time I was a Buddhist and Shintoist. Since there are more than 8 million gods in Shintoism, I was constantly searching to understand who God was and why he spared my life."*

"After the war," he said," *I was called as a witness in the war crime trials. Bitterness swelled in my heart against Americans who were punishing Japanese for alleged war crimes. I decided to search for accounts of atrocities committed by Americans on Japanese prisoners. I contacted an old friend, Lt Ranegasaki, who had been imprisoned in a hospital in Utah. I asked him how he was treated, expecting to hear tales of torture and agony.*

"But, instead, I was told of an 18 year-old girl, Margaret Covel, who had gone out of her way to be an angel of mercy. Margaret was the daughter of missionary parents, who had taught in the Baptist Seminary in Japan before the war. When the war began, they fled to the Phillipines and were later captured and shot as spies by the Japanese."

Fuchida said, *"When Margaret first learned of her parent's death, her heart filled with hatred for the Japanese. Later, however, she learned that just before her parents died, they prayed for her and for the forgiveness of the Japanese. Her attitude gradually changed until she was able to treat Japanese prisoners with Christian love and kindness. Instead of atrocities, I found Christian love,"* he said.

"When I returned to Tokyo, I was handed a Gospel Tract by a missionary, which told the story of Jacob de Shazer and how he had found God by reading the Bible.

Jacob de Shazer was one of those shot down over Japan in the *"Doolittle Raid"*. He was captured and imprisoned by the Japanese and was sure that his life was near its end. He saw two of his buddies beheaded and another die of slow starvation. During the long months of imprisonment his hatred of the Japanese burned like an unquenchable fire in his bosom.

Jacob de Shazer was an atheist. He ridiculed the weaklings that had to depend upon some god as a crutch, especially the goody-goody Christians. But with death staring him in the face at any moment and his arrogant feelings of self-sufficiency gone, he began to recall some of the things he had heard about Christianity.

Boldly, he asked his jailers if they could get him a Bible. At first they laughed boisterously as at a good joke, grew ugly, and warned him to stop making a nuisance of himself. But he kept asking. A year-and-a-half later, May 1944, a guard finally brought him a Bible, flung it at him, and said, *"Three weeks you have. Three weeks, and then I take away."* True to his word, in three weeks the guard took the Bible away and de Shazer never saw it again.

However, in those three weeks of intensive searching, meditating, and delving into the meaning of life and humanity's ultimate destiny, a change came about. He fell on his knees in his prison cell and prayed. He prayed to a God he wasn't even sure existed. In a moment all his doubts vanished. He felt the touch of God's presence. He had a personal encounter with Jesus.

He was released from captivity when the war ended and returned home. In 1948 Jacob de Shazer, his wife, and infant son were on their way back to Japan as missionaries.

Fuchida continued, *"So I purchased a Bible and began to read it. As I read of the love of God and the expression of that love by Jesus dying on the cross for me, I found what I had been searching for. I met the One I had been searching for, Jesus."*

When Fuchida finished his testimony, with tears in his eyes, he asked our forgiveness for Pearl Harbor. Most of us were veterans. Some had fought the Japanese and seen their buddies die. One was the son of missionary parents that had died in the Bataan death march.

In that upper room of a Los Angeles cafeteria, we all dropped to our knees and with arms around each other and tears streaming down our faces, prayed for Japan and America and one another.

All because of Jesus.

CHAPTER 26

MAN'S JUSTICE BRINGS GOD'S MERCY

U. S. Army Chaplain, Major Henry Gerecke, had been appointed spiritual advisor to 15 of Hitler's top men—the *"war criminals"* of the Nuremberg Trials. His story as recounted in Frederick Grossmith's book, *"The Cross and the Swastika"*, is a story of selfless courage, genuine caring love, and demonstrates the miraculous power of God's saving grace.

When the proposition first came to him that he become the chaplain to the indicted Nazis, Gerecke was shaken and perplexed. He wrestled within himself, *"How can a humble preacher, a one-time farm boy, make any impression on the disciples of Adolph Hitler?"*

Now that the war was over, he looked forward to returning to America after years of separation from his wife and family. Now, he was being asked to sacrifice his personal considerations to minister to some of the most hated and feared men in the world.

Gerecke reflected later, *"I had plenty of reasons for bitterness toward these men. I had been at the concentration camp in Dachau, where my hand had been smeared with human blood seeping through a wall. My oldest son, although he survived the fighting, had been literally ripped apart."*

"But slowly the men in prison at Nuremberg became to me—not war criminals but—but simply lost souls whom I was being asked to help. I determined as never before to hate the sin but love the sinner."

Gerecke made up his mind that by the grace of God he would bring the gospel of Jesus Christ to these hated and feared men.

The world might write off these Nazi leaders as hopeless, but he knew that through the cross, forgiveness is possible for anyone. Years later, he admitted that as he began his rounds, *"I was terribly frightened. How could I say the right thing—and say it in German?"*

The first one he visited was German Foreign Minister Joachim von Ribbentrop. Arrogant and snobbish, he made no attempt to conceal his indifference at the sight of an American army chaplain entering his untidy cell. An unfriendly man, disliked even by his colleagues, Ribbentrop had been one of Hitler's *"strong boys."* He was anti-Semitic to the core, considering Jews a useless breed.

But Ribbentrop's indifference seemed friendly in comparison with the sharpness of Rudolf Hess (*who died at 93 in Spandau Prison*). *"Would you care to attend chapel services"*, Gerecke asked. *"No,"* Hess replied with a scowl. *"I expect to be extremely busy preparing my defense."*

"I dreaded meeting the flamboyand egoist, Hermann Goering, more than any of the others, recalled Gerecke." When the chaplain entered his cell, Goering, who had been head of the German Luftwafe and one of Hitler's right hand men, jumped up and clicked his heels. *"Will you come in and spend some time with me?"* Goering said with warmth. *"I heard you were coming, and I'm glad to see you."*

Field Marshal Wilhelm Keitel, Chief of the German High Command, had given unquestioning obedience to Adolph Hitler, whom he considered to be a military genius. As Gerecke entered his cell, he noticed that he was reading. *"What are you reading?"* he asked in an interested manner. *"My Bible,"* Keitel answered softly. *"I know from this book that God can love a sinner like me."*

Immediately Gerecke thought this man must be a phony. *"But the longer I listened to him, the more I felt he might be sincere."* Keitel knew his chances of dodging the hangman's noose were slim. *"He knelt beside his cot,"* Gerecke later wrote, *"and read a portion of Scripture. Then he folded his hands, looked heavenward, and began to pray. I've never heard a prayer like that one. He spoke patiently of his many sins and pleaded for mercy by reason of Christ's sacrifice for him."*

A tiny chapel was improvised consisting of two cells with the wall between them knocked out. Its only furniture was a small altar, an organ, and chairs for those attending. On Sunday November 18, 1945, Gerecke preached in this sparse setting to 13 of the Third Reich's most feared leaders. Only Rosenberg and Hess stayed away.

Following that first service, Fritz Sauckel, former Plenipotentiary General for the Allocation of Labor, requested Gerecke to visit him. In his cell, Sauckel knelt beside his bed, and unafraid and unashamed, he prayed the sinner's prayer, *"God be merciful to me a sinner."* Sauckel's confession of his sins—which were many—*"mirrored the agony of a repentant soul,"* chaplain Gerecke said. At the trial he was described as *"the greatest and cruelest slaver since the pharaohs of Egypt."* Yet, God in His mercy, and amazing grace, brought unmerited forgiveness into Sauckel's life. He was a new man in Christ!

Ribbentrop remained friendly as long as the chaplain avoided the subject of salvation in Christ. But Goering ridiculed the idea of inspired Scripture.

The long trial ended on August 31, 1946. The eight judges went into secret session to consider their verdicts. During this quiet time, wives were allowed to visit their husbands in prison. Often the prisoners' children stayed in Gerecke's office on visiting days. Goering's wife, Emmy, urged her daughter, Edda, to talk to the chaplain.

"I asked the little girl if she said her prayers," Gerecke recalled, *"and she replied," "I pray every night "And how do you pray?" "I kneel by my bed and look up to heaven and ask God to open my daddy's heart and let Jesus in."*

Goering had attended 70 chapel services, but nothing seemed to touch him. His wife told him what his daughter had said to the chaplain. *"For the first time I saw tears in his eyes,"* recalled Gerecke. But that night Goering committed suicide by swallowing a capsule of potassium cyanide.

With Goering's suicide, von Ribbentrop headed the list as the first to be executed. As he stood under the gallows, Gerecke remembered, *"he turned to me—and my heart still warms to think of it—and said, "I'll see you again. I now know that God through Christ can love even a sinner like me."*

"For God so loved the world that He gave His only begotten Son that whosoever believeth in Him should not perish but have everlasting life." (John 3:16) The whosoever includes everyone—even murderers—*(for such was Moses, David and Paul)*. *"For all have sinned and come short of the glory of God."* (Rom. 3:23)

CHAPTER 27

BILLY GRAHAM, EVANGELIST TO THE WORLD

It was 1949. In a huddle of tents on the corner of Washington and Hill in downtown Los Angeles, a 30 year old evangelist named Billy Graham launched a crusade that over the next 50 years would change the lives of millions.

When 250,000 gathered in Central Park, New York City, to hear Billy Graham, it was said to be the largest religious gathering in the history of the North-American continent. It was the beginning of his second crusade in that city after 34 years. He had just returned from holding a school of evangelism in Moscow and audiences with both Gorbachev and Yeltsin.

Year after year Graham has been voted as among the top 10 most admired men in the world. He has avoided the scandals that have marred the ministries of so many televangelists.

Billy Graham has been through the years, the trusted confidante of presidents, kings, and world leaders, around the world. He has been a spiritual advisor to every American President since Truman. He has led in prayer at both the Republican and Democratic Conventions and is usually called on to give the Invocation at the Presidential Inaugurations.

In years past, Graham has been approached by both the Republican and Democratic parties to run for President, but choses rather to continue preaching, uncompromisingly, the simple gospel of Biblical Christianity and introduce people from almost every nation on earth to a personal, life-changing relationship with the King of Kings and Lord of Lords.

Political leaders in high places, movie and TV stars, university presidents, and corporate executives, as well as, gangsters, drug addicts, alcoholics, and prostitutes have had their lives made over through the power of Christ as they have heard about being *"born again"* through Billy's messages.

During the 1957 New York Crusade in Madison Square Garden, two million people attended, and it was extended from six to 16 weeks. In 1957, a church official warned Catholics away from the crusade, but in 1991, Cardinal John J. O'Connor of New York encouraged his flock to participate.

Though a Southern Baptist, Billy Graham says, *"I love everybody equally, and I have no problem in fellowship with anybody who says that Jesus Christ is Lord."*

When I first met Billy, many years ago, and had the privilege of serving as one of his Crusade counselors, I was especially impressed by his genuine spirit of humility. He has hob-nobbed with Kings and Potentates and could be a millionaire many times over, but he isn't. He receives a very modest salary, in the tens of thousands, not millions. Everything else, goes back into the ministry of spreading the gospel of Jesus Christ.

He has preached before hundreds of millions of people in most of the nations of the world. And it all began in Los Angeles.

The night Stuart Hamblen walked forward to declare his faith in Christ, a maid employed at the San Simeon castle of publisher William Randolph Hearst was in the audience. She knew her boss was a Hamblen fan and she reportedly told him what had happened. The next day Hearst sent a two-word telegram to the managing editor of the Los Angeles Examiner: *"Puff Graham."* Hearst's editors splashed the evangelist's story across their Sunday pages. And today Billy Graham is news wherever he goes, whether to Paris, Berlin, London, Nairobi, Addis Ababa, Rio de Janeiro, Prague or Moscow.

Stuart Hamblen was a Texas cowboy-singer who made several

fortunes with music and race horses, and almost dissolved everything in alcohol. One day at the track, after pocketing a particularly fat purse at Santa Anita, the notorious mobster, Mickey Cohen, approached him as he was getting in his car. He asked for a good tip on a sure thing for the next day. He said, *"I got $5,000 to put on one of your nag's noses. I'll make it worth your while."*

Hamblen reached inside the glove compartment, and in one swift motion yanked out a 45 and pointed it at the gangster. *"Look Mr. Cohen, if you don't blow out of here, I'll blow your brains out. Is that clear?"* Cohen blanched and blinked; his jowls quivered. He turned and walked away. Hamblen never heard from him again.

Out of curiosity and at the urging of his wife, Hamblen went to hear Billy Graham in that leaky tent on Washington and Hill. Although he promised to go only once, he kept going back. He came under such conviction for his sins one night that he felt like storming up to the platform and shutting that man up. But he kept coming back.

Hoping to escape his nagging conscience, he took the weekend off to relax on a bear-hunting excursion. But early in the evening of the first night he became feverish and sick. At three in the morning he went looking for Billy Graham. He found the evangelist checked in at a cheap hotel in a drab section of town.

"What are you doing to me?" he roared at the preacher, whom he had roused from bed. *"I haven't been able to sleep or eat. I've been sick."*

"We've been praying for you," Graham answered. Hamblen trembled as he listened to Billy explain the meaning of salvation. Looking him straight in the eye, Billy continued, *"You're the only one who can do anything for yourself, Stuart".* When Hamblen asked Graham to pray with him, the young preacher answered, simply, *"I don't think you are ready."*

"I could have belted him, I was so mad," Hamblen recalled when giving his testimony. After a few moments of silence, he said, falling to his knees, *"I'm ready, Billy. Please pray with me."* Graham knelt beside him. Together they prayed.

"It was like a rain of lamb's wool falling around me," Stuart Hamblen said, *"I was like a shivering man coming into a warm place out of a blizzard."*

He went home that morning feeling new and changed. He passed bars, open and inviting, without even a thought of going inside. When he put his hands in his pockets to warm them from the early morning cold, and found a pack of cigarettes, he threw it away without a qualm for his thirty-year habit.

He went on with his radio program and it continued to be a success. He joined the church, attended regularly and read a chapter of the Bible daily. It wasn't until he sold his stable of horses that he made news all over again. *"I didn't have to do it,"* he said, *"I sold my stable because I didn't want to encourage a poor, working guy to throw his money away on horses when it rightfully should have gone for the family groceries."*

The whiskey drinking stopped with the suddenness of a tap being turned off. There were times when he could hardly believe it. But he knew he would never touch the stuff again.

The *"Duke"*, John Wayne, and Stuart Hamblen were buddies. For many of the great Wayne horse operas, Hamblen served as the star's stunt man, standing in for him on all his dangerous riding and fighting scenes. When Wayne heard about the *"new"* Hamblen he wouldn't believe it. *"Hell, Stuart,"* he said, *"you've been drinking so long you're practically embalmed. What's the secret?"*

"It's no secret what God can do," Hamblen answered. Almost immediately upon saying those words, he knew he had just spoken the first line of a new song. *"The chimes of time ring out the news; Another day is thru. Someone slipped and fell. Was that someone you? You may have longed for added strength, your courage to renew. Do not be disheartened, for I bring hope to you. It is no secret what God can do. What He's done for others, He'll do for you. With arms wide open, He'll pardon you. It is no secret what God can do."*

CHAPTER 28

ELVIS STILL LIVES IN ROCK'N'ROLL

Jan. 8, 1935 there was born into the home of Vernon and Gladys Presley in the poorest white neighborhood of East Tupelo, Mississippi—Elvis Aaron Presley. Although *Elvis still lives in the hearts of his fans,* he died when only 42 on Aug. 16, 1977 of heart failure as a result of a (*prescription*) drug overdose.

A true Elvis fan, Carol Frazer, at 17, worked tirelessly to have a street named after Elvis. Her efforts were finally realized, when a street in suburban New Orleans was named *"Elvis Place."* Miss Frazer said she was so excited she didn't know what to do. Probably, go to an Elvis movie. But she has seen them all: *"Love Me Tender",* 107 times, *"Loving You",* 110 times, *"King Creole",* 91 times, and *"Jailhouse Rock,"* 79 times.

Carol moved from New Orleans to be near Elvis. She lived in a tiny Memphis flat with her mother, plus twelve scrapbooks about Elvis, 40,000 pictures of him, and a man-size cardboard replica of him overlooking her bed.

Elvis impersonators by the thousands seek to keep his memory alive and cash in on his undying fame. The United Press International in London reported that Elvis Presley was about to make his British debut—strumming his guitar and belting out rock-and-roll songs at a factory canteen. It was a 35-year-old Burmese immigrant.

His name was Narinder Singh until he had it legally changed to Elvis Presley. *"I thought it would help my career as a performer",* he said.

Although the real Elvis died of an overdose of prescription drugs, he hated alcohol—his mother, Gladys, died an early death because of it. He boasted that he took only legal drugs. Few in history have made such a tremendous impact on our culture, especially the *"Baby Boomer"* generation.

Much has been written about the *"King of Rock 'n' Roll"*, but little about his religious leanings and beliefs that so influenced his life.

One who knew Elvis intimately was his stepbrother, Rick Stanley. He was one of the last to see Elvis alive. In his book, *"Caught in a Trap"*, Rick tells of Elvis's search for meaning and love in his life, though he seemingly had everything that would bring happiness and a life of contentment.

Rick Stanley became Elvis Presley's little brother in 1960 at the age of five when his mother married Vernon Presley after the death of Gladys. In the next nine years, Rick grew up at Graceland and became Elvis's best friend. In 1969, Elvis asked Rick to join him on tour, and he was Elvis's personal assistant until the day Elvis died.

Elvis was not only Rick's big brother, he was his hero. When Elvis died, Rick's whole world came crashing down. Like many close to Elvis and in the Rock 'n' Roll scene, Rick was hooked not just on *"prescription drugs"*, but the hard stuff. He left Memphis after the funeral for Hollywood to take a job with a television crew. He joined the Hollywood party scene and was well on his way to destroying himself with cocaine and Quaaludes.

While in high school in Memphis, Rick had met and become enamored with a beautiful young lady, a cheerleader, Robyn Moye. Although, at first, it was a *"turn-off,"* she was the kind of *"good Christian girl"* his mother had always advised he needed. While on the road with Elvis he would call her. She was always happy, her voice full of enthusiasm. She was easy to talk to and they developed a close friendship.

She started asking Rick to go to church with her. Rick always said no. He asked her to go to bed with him. She always said no.

She was different. Though it wasn't *"cool"* for his crowd to be friends with such a *"Jesus freak"*, something kept drawing him back.

One night at one of the Hollywood parties, Rick colapsed and almost died from a drug overdose. Coming to, his first thought was to call Robyn, who had since moved to Florida with her parents. Hearing the desperation in his voice, she invited him to visit her and her family On the way to her home from the airport, Rick unloaded all the sordid details about his drug addiction.

She listened attentively until his voice broke and he began to sob. Compasionately, she said, *"Rick, what you need is Jesus—He'll give you strength to overcome your addiction".* She invited him to go to church with her that night. In desperation he agreed to go.

Jay Zinn, who had been a *"surfer"*, was the preacher. That night he preached on the text, *"Enter in at the narrow gate; for wide is the gate, and broad is the way, that leadeth to destruction, and many there be who go that way."* (Matt. 7:13) It seemed that the preacher was talking especially to him, and he knew he was on the road to destruction.

At the close of his message, Jay asked for those who wanted to accept Christ to raise their hands. Rick's hand shot up almost before he realized it. Talking to the pastor after the service, he prayed for God's forgiveness and that He would renew his life and make Jesus as real to him as He seemed to be to Robyn and this *"surfer"*, now a preacher.

Rick testifies, *"Suddenly, unexpectedly, miraculously, it happened! I felt waves of warm pure love that overflowed and filled my spirit and body. The incredible sense of forgiveness was beyond description. It was like a weight lifted from me. Lights seemed to burn brighter. Sounds were clearer. Later, when I met Robyn at the car, I realized that I no longer had any desire to do drugs. Or even smoke cigarettes. These addictions had been lifted from me."*

Rick Stanley married his best friend, Robyn Moye, that same year, 1978. A high school drop out, at age 24 he finally received his high school diploma. He went on to Bible College and Seminary.

Since 1978, as a Southern Baptist evangelist, he has given his testimony and preached in thousands of churches and high schools throughout the country. He often gives his testimony at Billy Graham Crusades around the world. He has appeared on *"20/20"*, *"Tom Snyder," "Good Morning America,"* and *"Larry King."* His story was featured in *"People"* magazine

He, who once served the *King of Rock 'n' Roll,* now serves the *King of Kings.*

CHAPTER 29

DRUGS, ROCK & ROLL, AND THE JESUS REVOLUTION

The babies born just after World War II came booming into the '60s and nearly caused a national nervous breakdown. Freedom rides and civil rights demonstrations. Black Power and clenched fists. Radical politics, peace marches, draft card burnings, campus take overs. Hippies and Hell's Angels, Drugs, Sex., Ear-splitting Rock Music, Violence, Strange affairs with the Occult. *"Playboy"* publisher Hugh Hefner marketed a philosophy of sexual hedonism, and *"If it feels good, do it"* became the watchword of the *"Baby Boom"* generation.

The *"Beatles"* hit the scene with an aggressive beat, wild platforming, and far-out appearances. Millions of kids bought the entire package—music, looks, and all. It was a passport to identity, a total-life language that expressed their disaffection with tradition. And—to the delight of the young—it reactivated the ulcers of parents who had agonized through the gyrations of Elvis Presley's *"Rock 'n' Roll"* of the '50s.

The Beatles had scarcely landed in America in 1964 before Mick Jagger and the Rolling Stones were nipping at their heels for the popularity crown. Meanwhile above the din and frenzy of hard and softrock, *"Leftist"* oriented dissenters and young idealists popularized the *"Folk song"* that knocked the status-quo. Bob Dylan, Woody Guthrie, Joan Baez, Peter, Paul, and Mary, Pete Seeger.

"*Blowing in the Wind,*" and "*Where Have All the Flowers Gone?*" told of their disenchantment.

In the mid-'60s Bob Dylan led in tieing the spirit of "folk" to the beat of "rock." Then came LSD and acid rock. Wild, freaky groups, stoned on stage. Screaming, pulsating sounds, weird electronics, images of erotica. Strobes, whirling colors, and flash-on films. Pro-drug songs made the Top 40 lists. *"Transcendent togetherness,"* Newsweek described the 1969 Woodstock event. *"Orgies,"* pronounced millions of outraged adults. Drugs silenced Jimi Hendrix, Janis Joplin and even the King, Elvis Presley, forever and were wrecking the lives of thousands.

The mood began to change. *Disillusionment. Despair. Meaninglessness.* Baby Boomers were asking, *"Is there not more to life?"* A pretty blonde on drugs told a CBS television reporter that she lived constantly with suicidal thoughts.

It was in the midst of this, that the Jesus Movement came on the scene. *"I just couldn't believe it was the real thing. Hippies reading the Bible and praying? Yet there they were—in the storefront coffeehouse, some ministers had opened near the intersection of Haight and Ashbury in San Francisco,"* said Ed Plowman, editor, "Christianity Today" and former Pastor of Park Presidio Baptist Church in San Francisco. *"Drugs didn't seem to matter anymore. They said Jesus Christ had given them a better high (euphoria). They spoke freely of their new love for God. They loved the Bible. They loved each other."* It was 1967.

The Jesus Movement traces its beginning to Ted Wise. He had the dubious distinction of having tripped out on some of the first black market LSD in Haight Ashbury. Before that, he had been on heroin and "speed". He and his wife Elizabeth lived in a commune in San Francisco before the public heard about communes. When marriage troubles worsened, Elizabeth—high on acid—went to the First Baptist Church across the Golden Gate Bridge in Mill Valley and asked the congregation to pray for Ted. She had become a Christian at age 12 at a Mt. Hermon Bible conference but went Ted's way after marriage. Now she wanted to come back to Christ.

Ted's first LSD trips did not turn out the way he had expected. *"I went into the palace looking for the prince on the throne,"* he recalls, *"but discovered only the rat in the basement."* The rat was himself. One day he picked up a stray Bible, began reading the New Testament, and in 1966 he quietly committed his life to Christ.

In 1971 *"Look"* magazine did a feature article on the *"Jesus movement"* phenomenon. A small church, Calvary Chapel of Costa Mesa, had skyrocketed in attendance from 150 to thousands in just two years. In 1970 alone 4,000 prayed to receive Christ and more than 2,000 were baptized in the Pacific Ocean. Most of the converts were those that many churches had rejected as hopeless, drug-crazed, long-haired hippies.

It all began with Lonnie and Connie Frisbee, who had moved to Costa Mesa from San Francisco and the Christian commune in Haight-Asbury, founded by Ted Wise and others. They opened *"The House of Miracles"* which was sponsored by the church. The rest is history. *"Look"* photographers, Jack and Betty Cheetham, were sent to photograph the Jesus movement. They were so impressed with what they saw that they too became Christians.

"Betty and I wanted what those kids had," said Jack. *"We had never found such love and joy before. Things hadn't been going right for us, and we were on a hate trip. The kids explained about Jesus and got us into the Bible. One night Betty and I went back to our room and invited Jesus into our lives. Now we have an inner peace we had never known possible."*

Ensnared by drugs, most had tried everything to escape the chains of addiction, but to no avail. But now, through Christ, the chains fell away. The Jesus movement became worldwide news.

One day in 1970, Paul Stookey, of *"Peter, Paul and Mary"* fame, showed up barefooted with his guitar on the Berkeley campus of the University of California. It was during a period of SDS disruptions. A huge crowd of students and street people from nearby

Telegraph Avenue pressed in around him. As Paul, no stranger to leftist causes, spoke of recent personal struggles in a desperate search for truth, the SDS agitators marched off to protest against the ROTC.

Paul said he had tried LSD and eastern religion, then finally sought out counsel from his folksinger friend, Bob Dylan. Dylan had recently become a Christian and he suggested he read the Bible. Paul took the advice. A short time later, following a performance in Abilene, Texas, a student talked with him backstage about Christ. *"Things were beginning to add up,"* he said.

"I went back to my motel room that night and got down on my knees," he told the hushed crowd. *"I prayed and asked Jesus to come into my life. He did, and I wept for joy the next 15 minutes."* He concluded with a challenge to others to follow his path to Jesus if they really wanted to discover truth in life and what living was all about.

Veteran *"Time"* reporter Kirsten Prager, a hard-bitten analyst who hadn't been in church since he was 15, helped with that magazine's June, 1971, cover story on the Jesus Revolution. *"After you've interviewed a while you get the feeling that these people are not into another `trip'. It is more than a fad,"* Prager said. Southern Baptist evangelist, Billy Graham, says, *"If it's all just a fad,—it's a good one."*

For over a quarter-century the Jesus revolution, crossing denominational lines, has touched the lives of millions of the baby-boomer generation and their children. Having experienced the failure of drugs and sexual promiscuity to satisfy, most have come full circle back to the conservative, traditional values held by their American forefathers for centuries. They still love the beat of Rock n Roll, but the lyrics lift up Christ rather than drugs and sex. Like the spiritual revivals that swept the American colonies before the birth of our nation, emphasis is placed on having an experiential relationship with Christ (being born again) and the absolute authority of the Bible as God's Word. *They have found that only Jesus truly satisfies.*

CHAPTER 30

ASTRONAUTS IN SPACE FEEL GOD'S PRESENCE

It was a spectacular and unforgetable moment in history when the world held its collective breath and prayed, as three men from America did the seeming impossible—landing on the moon.

When the pads of the Apollo 11 lunar module settled on the surface of the moon, we all breathed a sigh of relief as we heard the reassuring words, *"The Eagle has landed."*

We watched on our black and white TVs with anxious anticipation as Neil Armstrong exited the module and climbed down the ladder to cautiously set foot where no man had set foot before, on the surface of the moon. With millions upon millions of other viewers around the world we heard echoed forth those famous words, *"One small step for a man, one giant step for mankind."*

We watched with pride, as Neil Armstrong and Buzz Aldrin planted an American flag on the surface of the moon. Someone said, *"At least, no one will be able to burn that flag. There's no oxygen."*

N.A.S.A. scientists were concerned that a lunar ship might sink into vast amounts of cosmic dust which should have accumulated if the moon was billions of years old. It is known that there is essentially a constant rate of cosmic dust particles from space gradually settling to the earth and moon's surface. Hans Pettersson in *Scientific American* estimates that it amounts to 14 million tons per year.

If the earth and the moon are five billion years old as thought necessary to evolutionary theory, there should be a layer of meteoric dust (*with a high content of nickel and iron—rare in the earth's crust*) of at least 182 feet. Since there is no atmosphere on the moon and no erosion, as on earth, vast amounts of dust was expected.

N.A.S.A.'s fears were unfounded for they found less than an inch of such dust on the surface of the moon, suggesting the age of the moon to be not billions of years but thousands as the Bible suggests.

It was expected, also, (*assuming that life comes about by chance from dead matter when given billions of years to do so*) that there would be some form of primitive, bacterial life on the moon. But the moon was found to be absolutely sterile and devoid of any form of life.

Some years ago thousands of people responded to an ad in a Tucson newspaper offering deeds to 1,000 acre lots on the moon for $4.98. *What a bargain!* And there's a long list of people willing to pay a fortune to take a trip to the moon.

As wonderful as living on the moon might be, I haven't signed up yet. I'm afraid I would miss too many things on this earth. Imagine a baseball game on the moon. Each team would have to have dozens of outfielders scattered over a huge field, stirring up the dust. When a batter connected, the ball would fly a quarter of a mile or more. The base runner would be so light, that with a 30 foot stride, he would reach first base with only three steps.

The poor pitcher would have to rely on his straight ball, because without air on the moon, he couldn't pitch a curve. On the other hand the shortstop would be able to jump 20 feet into the air to snag an infield fly. The fans wouldn't have much fun, either; they couldn't holler at the umpire, for it takes air to make a sound, no matter how loud we yell.

The first close-up glimpse we got of the moon was on Christmas eve, 1968. Three astronauts aboard Apollo 8 were the first to escape the environs of the Earth and reach the Moon. Somewhere above the forbidding landscape of the Moon, the voices of Frank Borman, James Lovell, and William Anders carried to earth dwellers a Christmas message. It was a message welling up in their hearts and minds as they looked out on the fathomless reaches of the universe and back at the magnificently beautiful and shining blue sphere of the earth.

Overwhelmed with the feeling of the nearness of God's presence and realizing, as never before, the omnipotence and omniscience of the Creator who spoke it all into existence, they brought an unannounced and surprising message. It was Genesis 1:1-10.

"In the beginning, GOD created the heaven and the earth," intoned Anders as the astronauts' TV camera flashed back remarkable pictures of the deeply shadowed lunar landscape. Borman closed the lunar telecast with the words: *"Good night, good luck, a Merry Christmas, and God bless all of you upon the good earth."*

The trio then closed the moonship's telecast and began preparations for the successful blast out of lunar orbit to return to the *"grand oasis in the vastness of space, earth."*

Flushed with the *"victory"* of having the Bible and prayer *censored* out of America's schools, atheist and *Marxist,* Madalyn Murray O'Hair, filed a *petition of protest,* claiming 20,000 signatures. But immediately, *millions* of Americans flooded the mails with letters *"protesting her protest."* The U.S. Post Office issued a commemorative stamp of the Apollo 8 flight with the words, *"In the beginning God..."* On Feb. 5, 1970, a microfilm packet containing Genesis 1:1 in 16 languages and a complete Bible were deposited on the Moon by Apollo 14 LEM Commander, Edgar Mitchell.

Isaac Newton, father of the science of modern-day Physics, and without whose discoveries, the space age would be impossible, made a replica of the solar system in miniature. In the center was the sun with its retinue of planets revolving around it.

A fellow scientist entered Newton's study one day, and exclaimed, *"My! what an exquisite thing this is! Who made it?"* *"Nobody!"* replied Newton to the questioner. *"You must think I am a fool,"* said the questioner. *"Of course somebody made it, and he must be a genius."*

Laying his book aside, Newton rose from his chair, laid a hand on his friend's shoulder and said: *"This thing is but a puny imitation of a much grander system whose laws you and I know, and I am not able to convince you that this mere toy is without a designer and maker.*

"Yet, you profess to believe that the great original from which the design is taken has come into being without either designer or maker. Now tell me, by what sort of ridiculous reasoning do you reach such incongruous conclusions?"

Astronaut Jack Lousma says his experiences, *"reinforced my faith that there was a God who created the world. From what I've seen up there, it is clear that a Master Creator and Planner made it happen!"*

Colonel James B. Irwin is one of only twelve humans ever to have walked on the surface of the moon. As Lunar Module Pilot of the Apollo 15 mission, he lifted off from Cape Kennedy on July 26, 1971, and landed on the moon four days later for a record sixty-seven hour stay there.

In June 1979 Col. Irwin was invited to speak to a packed congregation in the Evangelical Baptist Church in Moscow. He told how his experience on the moon *changed* the whole course of his life as he had an especially close encounter with God.

"As we were fulfilling our scientific mission, I felt a special closeness of God in everything, and I prayed to Him often. I sensed a kind of direct communication with God and felt His presence more than I had ever felt it."

America's astronauts realized, as never before, how true are the words of the Psalmist: *"If I ascend up into heaven, thou art there; if I make my bed in sheol, behold, thou art there. If I take the wings of the morning, and dwell in the uttermost parts of the sea, Even there shall thy hand lead me, and thy right hand shall hold me."* (Ps. 139:8-10)

CHAPTER 31

EVOLUTION, IS IT FACT OR FAITH?

You probably won't read or hear about it in the national media, but a growing number of well known scientists and intellectuals are abandoning their faith in evolution.

Recent advances in biology and other sciences have dealt such heavy blows to evolution that one scientist said, *"This whole thing is coming apart at the seams."*

As reported by Thomas Woodward, Colin Patterson, Senior Paleontologist of the British Museum of Natural History, in 1981 started asking other scientists to tell him one thing they knew, as a proven fact, about evolution.

Lecturing to biologists at the American Museum of Natural History in New York City, he said, *"I tried that question on the geology staff at the Field Museum of Natural History and the only answer I got was silence.*

"I tried it on the members of the Evolutionary Morphology Seminar in the University of Chicago, a very prestigious body of evolutionists, and all I got there was silence. Eventually one person said, 'I do know one thing—it ought not to be taught in high school.'"

Patterson said, *"One day in 1980 I woke up and realized that all my life I had been duped into taking evolutionism as revealed truth in some way."* He said he had experienced *"a shift from evolution as knowledge to evolution as faith."*

He says one of the main reasons for his skepticism concerning evolution, as a scientific fact, is that there are no real transitional forms anywhere in the fossil record. *(Transitional fossels would be in-between forms, such as fish gradually developing arms and legs and turning into land animals.)*

Although Patterson still believes that evolution has occurred, he emphasizes that belief in creation or belief in evolution is equally a *faith* commitment.

Because of recent findings in genetics, molecular biology, and information science, a growing number of skeptics are also embracing the concept of an intelligent creator as the most plausible explanation of the origin of life. As scientists have studied in detail the intricacies of the cell—with its chemical factories and spiral-ladder molecules of DNA that record millions of bits of genetic information—many have started wondering how all this could have happened by chance, through natural processes.

British astronomer, Fred Hoyle, famous for his research on the origins of the universe, claims that believing the first cell originated by chance is like believing a tornado could sweep through a junkyard filled with airplane parts and form a Boeing 747. He believes, however, that the creator of these genes is not God, but some superintelligent, extraterrestrial life. He doesn't say how the extraterrestrial life came into being.

"Can a Christian accept the theory of evolution and still be a Christian?" The answer is *"Yes"*. Many very sincere and genuine Christians do believe that it was by the process of evolution, that God created us. *I was one of them.*

I attended a university, receiving a degree in Psychology and Philosophy, in which the theory of evolution was taught as *"scientific fact"* and the whole concept of God, and a supernatural creation as revealed in the Bible was ridiculed. Awed and overwhelmed by the *"irrefutable evidences"* given for evolution by the professors, I too accepted evolution as *"fact"*.

I was not told that it is impossible to prove scientifically any theory of origins. The very essence of the scientific method is based on observation and experimentation, and it is impossible to make observations or conduct experiments on the origin of the universe.

This point is conceded by British biologist, L. Harrison Matthews, in the foreword to the 1971 edition of Darwin's *"Origin of Species"*. He states:

"The fact of evolution is the backbone of biology, and biology is thus in the peculiar position of being a science founded on an unproved theory—is it then a science or a faith? Belief in the theory of evolution is thus exactly parallel to belief in special creation—both are concepts which believers know to be true but neither, has been capable of proof."

Scientists may speculate about the past or future but they can only actually observe the present. Obviously, then, the widespread assumption that evolution is an established fact of science is absolutely false.

I was not told that many distinguished scientists completely dismiss the concept of organic evolution in favor of Biblical creationism. For instance, Dr. John Grebe, director of basic and nuclear research for Dow Chemical Company, offered $1,000 to anyone who could produce just one clear proof of evolution. Dr. Grebe's challenge is not to be taken lightly. His credentials are extremely impressive, having over 100 patents and being responsible for the development of styrofoam, synthetic rubber, and Saran Wrap.

Co-holder of the 1945 Nobel Prize for developing penicillin, Sir Ernest Chain, stated: *"To postulate that the development and survival of the fittest is entirely a consequence of chance mutations seems to me a hypothesis based on no evidence and irreconcilable with the facts. It amazes me that evolution is swallowed so uncritically and readily, and for such a long time, by so many scientists without a murmur of protest."*.

Dr. Etheridge, world-famous paleontologist of the British Museum, has remarked: *"Nine-tenths of the talk of evolutionists is sheer nonsense, not founded on observation and wholly unsupported by facts. This museum is full of proofs of the utter falsity of their views. In all this great museum, there is not a particle of evidence of the trasmutation of species."*

Dr. Albert Fleischmann, of the University of Erlangen, has

written: *"I reject evolution because I deem it obsolete; because the knowledge, hard won since 1830, of anatomy, histology, cytology, and embryology, cannot be made to accord with its basic idea. The foundationless, fantastic edifice of the evolution doctrine would long ago have met with its long-deserved fate were it not that the love of fairy tales is so deep-rooted in the hearts of man."*

Somehow, I had to reconcile the *"scientific fact"* of evolution with the Bible. Perhaps, as *"theistic"* evolutionists believe, the process of evolution was the way God brought man and the material universe into being. But the more I studied about evolution and the more I studied the Bible the more I realized that the two cannot be reconciled nor harmonized. I couldn't simply hide my head in the sand as an ostrich and hope the problem would go away.

The whole concept of evolution is inconsistent with the God of the Bible. Evolution involves the development of innumerable misfits and extinctions, useless and even harmful organisms. If this is God's *"method of creation"* it is strange that He would use such haphazard, inefficient, wasteful processes, and take so long to do it. Surely the omniscient, omnipotent God of the Bible could do better. *"God is not the author of confusion"* (1 Cor. 14:33). Then, the idea of the *"survival of the fittest,"* whereby the stronger animals and races eliminate the weaker in the *"struggle for existence"* is flatly contradicted by the Biblical doctrine of love and unselfish sacrifice for others. Jesus said, *"Love your enemies, bless them that curse you, do good to them that hate you, and pray for them who despitefully use you, and persecute you, that ye may be the sons of your Father, who is in heaven..."* (Matt. 5:44,45)

In evolution, however, selfishness, violence, and the death and destruction of the weak is considered good and makes for upward progression.

Many maintain that Genesis is mainly myth and legend, and that it is filled with scientific and historical errors. However, if the writers of the New Testament were wrong about Genesis, they were probably wrong about other things. Jesus Christ, Himself, specifically quoted from Genesis 1 and 2 (in Matt. 19:4-6), accepting it as historically accurate and divinely authoritative. If Christ was a liar or ignorant of the facts, then He cannot be God and my Savior.

The Bible teaches plainly that there was no suffering and death before Adam sinned. *"Wherefore, as by one man, sin entered into the world and death by sin."* (Rom. 5:12). Death came into the world only when sin came into the world—not ages before, as evolution teaches. *"By man came death."* (1 Cor. 15:21).

Man is not an upward-evolving animal but, rather, a lost sinner under the condemnation of death. *"For as in Adam all die, even so in Christ, shall all be made alive."* (1 Cor. 15:22). If, as *"theistic"* evolution holds, death was God's way of creating from the beginning and not a result of man's sin, Christ's selfless sacrifice of Himself on the cross for our sins was a meaningless farce.

One of the many Russian scientists and intellectuals who have sought and received asylum in the West is Dr. Boris Dotsenko. Dotsenko attended the University of Ivov, receiving his first academic degree in physics and mathematics in 1949. He went to the University of Leningrad and obtained his doctorate at Moscow State University in 1954.

After working for three years in the prestigious Academy of Sciences of the USSR, on intercontinental and space rocket research, he moved to the Institute of Physics in Kiev, where he was eventually appointed Head of the Nuclear Laboratory.

He had been thoroughly indoctrinated in the Russian schools from early childhood in the theory of evolution and *"scientific atheism."* Karl Marx based his whole concept of communism and dialectic materialism on the theory of evolution. When communism took over in China, the first thing done, after killing most of the Christians, intellectuals, and property owners, who resisted, was to mandate crash courses (*not in Marxist communism*) but in Darwinian evolution. Dr. Dotsenko says, *"I, too absorbed it into the very marrow of my bones."*

However, something that bothered him, as he learned more

and more of science, was one of the most fundamental laws of nature, the Law of Entropy, which is concerned with the probable behavior of the particles (*molecules, atoms, electrons, etc.*) of any physical system. Put simply, this law states that, left to itself, any physical system will decay or run down (*just as a clock runs down*) in time and matter tends to become increasingly disorganized (*not more organized*).

(*One of the implications of this law is that the whole material world should have turned into a cloud of chaotic dust a long time ago, if the universe is billions of years old as claimed.*) Common sense and the Law of Entropy says it is impossible for a worm to make itself into a man; "*scientific evolution*" says, in a million years it can.

Dotsenko states, *"As I thought about all of that, it suddenly dawned on me that there must be a very powerful organizing force counteracting this disorganizing tendency within nature, keeping the universe controlled and in order. This force must be nonmaterial; otherwise, it too would become disordered. I concluded that this power must be both omnipotent and omniscient: therefore there must be a God—one God—controlling everything! I realized also that even the most brilliant scientists in the best equipped laboratories are still incapable of copying even the simplest living cell: God must be the Creator of life on Earth."*

While still in his teens, he related how he was at his grandfather's while recovering from pneumonia. He wandered into an old barn and fell asleep on a pile of hay. When he awoke, he discovered that he had slipped down between the hay and the back wall of the barn. There, by his feet, he saw some old papers.

Reaching down, he found a book, its pages yellowed with time. It was a Bible without a cover. It was the first one he had seen. He says, *"I was frightened. I knew that Christianity was frowned upon. Churches had been burned down or closed. Christian preaching had become a crime. I was intrigued, however. I hid the book under my shirt and sneaked back to my room."*

There he read more. The book opened to John 1:1—*"In the beginning was the Word, (Christ) and the Word was with God, and the Word was God...All things were made by him; and without him *was not anything made that was made."* It completely contradicted everything that he had been taught! It was a shocking experience for him and he never forgot it.

As he read on, he felt increasingly uncomfortable. He says, *"The Great Commandment of Jesus to love God and my neighbor as myself particularly frightened me. How could I love God and my neighbor as myself if God did not exist? I had been told that any enemy who does not surrender must be annihilated. I had learned that I had a responsibility to betray, not only my neighbor, but even my own family."*

While he was studying for his master's degree in Leningrad, he discovered another Bible in an unlikely place: the study of Dr. Jakov Frenkel, a Russian scientist of world renown. It impressed him greatly that this brilliant man who had the most intimate knowledge of the laws of nature, should keep the Bible openly in his library.

One day, he was called to Moscow, to the Central Committee of the Soviet Communist Party and was told that he was to be sent to Canada, as a senior member of the International Atomic Energy Agency. Two days later, he was in Canada, at the University of Alberta. When he began to unpack his luggage in his Edmonton motel room, he found a third Bible—this one placed there by the Gideons.

He testifies, *"My hands trembled as I lifted the Bible. It too opened to John 1:1, and my eyes again fell on the same words that struck me so forcibly twenty-two years before in the Ukrainian barn: "In the beginning was the Word..." Thereafter, I spent every available moment absorbing the Word of God. I devoured it like a starving man."* It not only satisfied his spiritual thirst, it answered his intellectual questions. He read, *"For by Him were all things created, that are in heaven, and that are in earth...And He is before all things, and by Him all things consist. (hold together). (Col. 1:16,17).*

In that motel room,. Boris Dotsenko, met the God he knew had to exist. The God who not only created the universe but holds it together, Jesus Christ. *"I quickly realized,"* he says, *"that my relationship with Jesus Christ was more important to me than my career, or even my beloved homeland and family. So I stayed in Canada and began teaching physics at several schools and universities."*

Dr. Werner von Braun was deputy director of the National Aeronautics and Space Administration. His scientific knowledge helped make possible America's Space Program. He was, also, a dedicated Christian.

At a Colorado governor's prayer breakfast, he said, *"The public has a deep respect for the amazing scientific advances made within our lifetime. But many who believe in God as Creator, as I do, have difficulty accepting Him as a personal God, who is interested, not only in the human race, but in the individual."* He continued, *"Man can know God only by His self-revelation in the person of Jesus Christ, as witnessed by Scripture."*

CHAPTER 32

LAND OF OPPORTUNITY AND THE SECOND CHANCE

"Now, in the one in a million case," said the sergeant, *"that the main parachute shouldn't open, just bear in mind, you have a reserve parachute. Just pull the hook on the right side. It will open gradually. Relax when you hit the ground. There will be no pain. There will be a station wagon there to take you back to the barracks."*

But one soldier still wasn't convinced. The sergeant got him to the door, however, and pushed him out *gently*. The young soldier yanked the cord, and nothing happened. Then he yanked the reserve hook and looked up, but again nothing happened. As he was plummeting down, with lightning speed to the ground, he said to himself, *"Now I'll just bet that station wagon won't be there either."*

A small town paper reported that a newcomer, who had moved there to escape the traffic and congestion of the city, was run over by the *Welcome Wagon*. As someone has said, *"If at first you don't succeed, welcome to the club."*

What's so great about America? In America we have the freedom and opportunity not only to succeed, but to fail. And if we fail, there waits, not a debtor's prison, but a second chance.

.The history books are filled with the biographies of *failures* who made good. From them we can learn the valuable lesson; that failure need not be fatal. Failure is never pleasant. It certainly isn't pleasant to lose a job, see a relationship falter, or fail a test. But, in

America, we have the freedom to keep on getting up one more time than we fell.

The first president of the United States—the father of our country—lost two-thirds of the battles he fought during the Revolutionary War. But George Washington won the war, founded a nation and succeeded, brilliantly, in spite of those failures.

When George Washington took command of the Continental Army in 1775, the 43-year-old general was a man rendered hopelessly unfit for military service by today's standards. He had suffered frequent attacks of smallpox, influenza, tubercular pleurisy, dysentery, and malaria. Despite his sickly condition, however, we have no record that Washington was ever incapacitated at all during the Revolutionary war.

Who failed more than Babe Ruth? In a baseball career that spanned 21 years, the immortal slugger hit 851 home runs, but he struck out 1,330 times! Until he retired in 1935, this famous *failure* was baseball's biggest attraction.

After Edison had experimented 10,000 times with his storage battery and still couldn't get it to work, a friend tried to comfort him. *"Why, I have not failed,"* Edison replied, *"I've just found 10,000 ways that won't work."*

Nearly deaf, with only three months of formal schooling, Thomas A. Edison patented more than 1,100 inventions. During his 60 years of reaching toward the unknown, Edison *failed* more than he succeeded.

A Springfield, Illinois lawyer was defeated for the state legislature by 23 votes in 1832; went into partnership with William F. Berry in a New Salem store but only got deeper in debt; proposed to Mary Owens who turned him down; sought the Whig party's nomination for Congress in 1843 and 1844, but failed to get it. He sought but failed to be appointed Commissioner of the General Land Office in 1849; and failed at a bid for the Senate. Finally, however, he was nominated for President and on the ballot in 1860 won his parties' nomination and the Presidency.

Abraham Lincoln failed more than he succeeded. His appearance was anything but charismatic. He was tall, skinny, and stooped. He grew a beard to cover pock marks on a less than handsome face. As a young midwestern lawyer, he suffered such deep depression that his friends thought it wise to keep all knives and razors from him. During this time he wrote, *"I am now the most miserable man living."* He was one of the most hated of men during the Civil War, resulting in his assassination. Yet, Abraham Lincoln preserved the Union, freed the slaves, and is considered one of America's greatest and most loved Presidents.

"Friends, I have forgotten all I had to say," confessed red-faced David Livingstone, as he got up to preach his first sermon. Humiliated, he hurriedly ran down the aisle and out into the darkness thinking he would never amount to anything. But David Livingstone went on to plant the gospel in Africa along with his heart. The rest of his body was buried with honors in Westminster Abbey.

Billy Sunday had a promising career in major league baseball, but he was enslaved by alcohol. *"I stumbled drunk into the arms of Jesus,"* Sunday confessed. After Jesus changed Sunday's life, this flamboyant Presbyterian evangelist preached to more than 100 million people and introduced multitudes to the same life changing power found in a personal relationship with Christ.

Jacob was a liar, a cheat, a deceiver. He cheated his brother Esau, out of his birthright, and had to flee for his life. He was in turn cheated by his uncle Laban out of seven years labor for the girl he loved, Rachel. He lost his favorite son, Joseph, who was sold into slavery by his jealous brothers. But Jacob became the father of the twelve tribes of Israel.

Moses killed an Egyptian taskmaster and had to flee into the desert. He lost all the privileges of being a Prince of Egypt and became a lowly shepherd in the desert for 40 years. He was slow of speech. But God called him to lead the children of Israel out of bondage in Egypt and at Sinai to give His law to His people.

King David looked upon Bathsheba to lust after her and committed adultery with her. He murdered her husband by having him sent to the front to be killed. But David repented when the prophet Nathan pointed out his sin, and one day Jesus the Son of David and David's Lord, will sit upon the throne of David.

Peter had walked with Jesus day and night for more than three years. He was ready to fight when Roman soldiers came to take Jesus away in the garden of Gethsemane. But when Jesus stood on trial before Pilate to be crucified, Peter denied his Lord; not once but three times. And yet after weeping bitter tears of repentance, Peter was used of God to preach a sermon on the Day of Pentecost that resulted in the salvation of 3,000 souls.

God loves *"failures"*. Not our failings, but those who fail. *"For all have sinned (missed the mark) and come short of the glory of God."* (Rom. 3:23) *"In this was manifested the love of God toward us, because that God sent his only begotten Son into the world, that we might live through Him."* (I John 4:9)

Towering above New York Harbor is the *Statue of Liberty*, a symbol of hope for oppressed peoples around the world. For over one hundred years, that stately lady, with freedom's torch held high, has welcomed refugees from across the seas. Inscribed on the pedestal of this imposing monument are these words:

"Give me your tired, your poor, Your huddled masses yearning to breath free, The wretched refuse of your teeming shore, Send these, the homeless, tempest-tossed, to me: I lift my lamp beside the golden door."

Each year when we celebrate America's Independence Day, the 4th of July, with parades and picnics, and firewdrks, we remind ourselves of the greatness of our country and especially its freedoms. Freedoms hard won by our forefathers, but so often taken for granted today.

With the collapse (at least for now) of communism in Russia and Eastern Europe, we tend to forget that the totalitarianism of communism is still in control of over one-fifth of the world's population in North Korea, Vietnam, Cuba and China with a population of over one billion.

Just a few years ago, we watched, spellbound, on our TVs as

one million peaceful, non-violent demonstrators clogged the streets of Tienanmen Square, Beijing, China, crying out for the freedoms we have enjoyed in America for over 200 years.

It was very evident that they had been inspired by the freedoms of America in their protests against their Communist masters. Tears welled up in my eyes as the students reverently carried through the crowd a replica of our Statue of Liberty. Before the eyes of the camera they flashed "V" for Victory signs and hoisted banners in both Chinese and English with the moving words of Patrick Henry, *"Give me liberty or give me death.!!"*

And there in the midst of that mass of humanity, was lifted up a ten-foot cross, carried by the pastor of one of the many thousands of underground, house churches, that had exploded into existence throughout China in recent years in spite of unrelenting persecution. Christians from other underground churches brought food from their own meager supply and distributed it among the students, and cared for those that had become ill because of the hunger-strike.

One reporter related how a student had confided to him of his disillusionment with communism. University students, many of them sons and daughters of the bureaucratic leadership of the Communist Party, are among the most privileged classes in China. They are thoroughly endoctrinated in atheistic, dialectic materialism, and yet this young man said, *"Is this all I have to live for...a better television or a bigger refrigerator? There has got to be more."*

It began to look for a while that the demonstrators for democracy were going to win the freedoms they cried out for. But it was not to be. Over night, the Army massacred thousands, firing into the crowds indiscriminately, and crushing them with tanks. In spite of the later denial by the Chinese government, the horror of it could not be erased from the minds and hearts of a world that had seen it graphicly portrayed before their eyes' on TV. Our hearts cried out, *"How could they do it?"*

Millions of immigrants, who could not tolerate the stifling air of tyranny, have responded to the invitation on the Statue of Liberty and made America their homeland. Too often, however, many have been disappointed because America's streets were not paved with gold as they expected. America is a land of *"opportunity"*, not *"heaven on earth"*.

In 1872 a certain business establishment posted the following rules on the bulletin board. *"(1) Office employees will daily sweep the floors, dust the furniture, shelves, and showcases. (2) Each day fill lamps, clean chimneys and turn wicks. Wash the windows once a week. (3) Each clerk will bring in a bucket of water and a scuttle of coal for the day's business. (4) Make your pens carefully. You may whittle your nibs to your individual taste. (5) This office will open at 7:00 a.m. and close at 9:00 p.m. daily, except on Sunday, on which day it will remain closed. Each employee is expected to spend Sunday attending church and contributing liberally to the cause of the Lord. (6) Men employees will be given an evening off each week for courting purposes, or two evenings a week if they go regularly to church. (7) After an employee has spent 13 hours of labor in the office, he should spend the time reading the Bible and other good books. (8) Every employee should lay aside from each pay a goodly sum of his earnings, so that he will not become a burden upon the charity of others."*

Down through the years, people around the world have tried to fix their economic problems with a multitude of *"isms."* Someone has tried to explain these different approaches as follows:

"Communism: You have two cows. The government takes both of them and gives you part of the milk.

Socialism: You have two cows. The government takes one and gives it to your neighbor.
Fascism: You have two cows. The government takes both cows and sells you the milk.
Nazism: You have two cows. The government takes both cows, then shoots you.
Bureaucracy: You have two cows. The government takes both of them, shoots one, milks the other, then pours the milk down the drain.

Capitalism: You have two cows. You sell one of them and buy a bull. More cows."

Unfettered *"free enterprise"* isn't perfect, but it's the best man has been able to come up with so far.

When God made man, he planted a garden in Eden and gave Adam the work of tending the garden. It was a paradise until Adam and Eve sinned in choosing to believe the lie of Satan and ate of the tree of knowledge of good and evil in rebellion against God.

As punishment for that rebellion, God cursed the earth so that it brought forth thorns and thistles, and Adam was forced to make his living by the *"sweat of his brow."* It is not labor that is a curse of God, but *"hard"* labor. It is a labor in the presence of the thorns and thistles of frustration and *"Murphy's Law."* *"If anything can go wrong, it will."*

But the Bible says there is coming a day when, *"there shall be no more curse: but the throne of God and of the Lamb shall be in it: and his servants shall serve him."* (Rev. 22:3)

And when, *"they shall beat their swords into plowshares, and their spears into pruninghooks, nation shall not lift up a sword against nation, neither shall they learn war any more. But they shall sit every man under his vine and under his fig tree:* (private property ownership and free enterprise) *for the mouth of the Lord of hosts hath spoken it."* (Micah 4:3,4)

Engraved on The United Nations Building in New York City is the Scripture quoted above. It is hoped by the wisdom of man, a New World Order (Globalism) will bring about world peace and prosperity for all.

The only problem is, the dream is not new. The dream of one world goes all the way back to the Tower of Bable, when Nimrod sought to build a one-world government. God, however, intervened, confounded their languages and scattered them over the face of the earth. Throughout history, Kings, and Emperors, and Dictators have sought to conquer the world and establish one world government. Whether it be a Nebuchadnezer, an Alexander the

Great, a Julius Caesar, a Charlemagne. a Napoleon, a Hitler, or a Stalin, all have tried, but failed.

When the Disciples asked Jesus about His coming again and the end of the world, he answered: "*...ye shall hear of wars and rumours of wars...nation shall rise against nation, kingdom against kingdom...All these are the beginning of sorrows...For then shall be great tribulation, such as was not since the beginning of the world to this time, no, nor ever shall be...Therefore be ye also ready: for in such an hour as ye think not the Son of man cometh.*" (Matt. 24:4,6-8,21,44)

Until that day, life is a struggle. But there is hope and help and strength for the one who labors in Christ. Jesus says, "*Come unto me, all ye that labor and are heavy laden, and I will give you rest. Take up my yoke and follow me; for I am meek and lowly in heart: and ye shall find rest unto your souls.*" (Matt. 11:28-29)

The picture is that of two oxen yoked together in a double yoke, pulling a common load. When we are united to Christ, yoked to Him, we pull the load together. And it's easy! *He does most of the pulling.*

George Washington Carver once asked God to tell him about the universe. According to Carver, the Lord replied, "*George, the universe is just too big for you to understand. Suppose you let Me take care of that.*"

Humbled, he replied, "*Lord, how about a peanut?*" The Lord said, "*Now, George, that's something your own size. Go to work on it and I'll help you.*" When Carver was done studying the peanut, he had discovered over 300 products that could be made with that little bit of God's universe.

Even as the *Statue of Liberty* gives an invitation to those burdened down with the bondage of the tyranny of men, so Jesus gives a gracious invitation to all those burdened down with the bondage of the tyranny of sin. "*If the Son, therefore, shall make you free, ye shall be free indeed.*" (John 8:36)

CHAPTER 33

WHAT EVER HAPPENED TO SIN?

There is a tradition to the effect that Noel Coward sent identical notes to twenty prominent men in London, saying, *"All is discovered. Escape while you can."* All twenty abruptly left town.

Even though we like to deny it, especially to ourselves, we all realize down deep in the depths of our hearts that we are guilty sinners.

Some years ago 7,000 psychologists jammed into Cincinnati for their annual convention. The University of Illinois' famed researcher, 0. Hobart Mowrer, declared, *"We psychologists have largely followed the Freudian doctrine that human beings are too good. And that,"* he went on to say, *"the patient has within him impulses, especially those of lust and hostility which he has been unnecessarily inhibiting. And health, we tell him, lies in recognizing and expressing these impulses...As a result, we have largely abandoned belief in right and wrong, virtue and sin."*

Sigmund Freud's psychoanalysis reflected his beliefs and opinions. His patients were mostly affluent and neurotic Viennese women. He was a student of Darwinian evolutionary theories and although Jewish, an atheist.

The conscience to Freud was a *learned response to taboos created by the tyrannical father type who became a tribal god, they called Jehovah.* Psychoanalysis became the *"in thing",* especially among those who could afford years of treatment. *It enabled the patient to blame his problems on his mother or society in general. It gave him an excuse to do whatever he felt like doing since there is no standard of right and wrong.*

Freudian psychoanalysis was discredited, however, among all but the most loyal followers and/or those who had spent thousands of dollars or more in training to become highly paid psychoanalysts.

In a study by Eysenck at the University of London, neurotic patients were divided 50/50 and it was found that those who underwent psychoanalysis had no better recovery rate than those who just lived life and saved the massive therapy fees. The recovery was the same, plus or minus a .02 percent statistical error factor.

Then came *behaviorism* and *"Behavior Modification"* which utterly rejected the theories of Freud as scientifically unfounded speculations and opinion. The most famous of the behaviorist school was B. F. Skinner of Harvard, inventor of the Skinner box.

Skinner announced that basically man was a *soulless* animal who had no free will, and no guarantee of meaning or happiness in life. Man was nothing but a machine to be manipulated by social engineering. Again there was no standard of right or wrong to be concerned about.

Rejecting the total materialism of behaviorism, Abraham Maslow and Carl Rogers then assured the world that there was meaning to life after all. *Humanistic Psychology* declared that people had free choice and were not just a random collection of molecules, but were rather part of a larger spiritual dimension. *"Feelgood"* psychology made its entrance.

Under Rogerian, non-directive therapy, and transactional analysis *(I'm okay, you're okay)* a gnawing conscience that convicted of sin and that one just might not be "*okay*", was selectively cut away by a scalpel of permissiveness. Conscience and guilt were like vestigial organs, no longer serving a useful function.

The conscience, it is said, is part of man's primitive brain, holding him back from full self-expression, from freedom, creativity, and joy. In client-centered therapy, the patient has all the answers within himself. Human nature is basically good and self-actualization can be achieved by a total non-judgmental self-acceptance and self-love. Then the unfathomable depths of human potential can be tapped.

Self-centeredness and selfishness; finding one's self and putting self first is supposedly the way to fulfillment. Hedonism and the unfettered pursuit of pleasure is okay, and freedom means you can do almost anything and *if it feels good you can do it. One's greatest responsibility is toward self, not others.*

For years, Psychologists, Sociologists, Educators, and Criminologists have insisted that the reason individuals and society have so many problems, is *low self-esteem.* Too often, instead of majoring on the 3 Rs, our Public Schools, major on trying to raise a child's self-esteem and *"feeling good about himself."* So much so, that "*self-esteemism*" has become a religion. If you're a criminal or having problems of any kind, its because you're a victim of society and you have low self-esteem; therefore, you're not responsible for your actions.

But "*lo and behold*" comes a recent "*Psychological Study*" that finds: Neo-Nazis, wife-beaters, KKK members and habitual criminals have one thing in common—*extremely high self-esteem.*

The Psychologists and Criminologists that conducted the study and published their findings in the *"Psychological Review"* were literally knocked off their learned props. It wasn't what they expected to find at all. Apparently, *"too much self-esteem is worse than too little".*

Our problems today are not because of man's low concept of himself, but of his low concept of God. Too many have dethroned God and put *"self"* on the throne, They feel no responsibility for their actions to anyone except themselves. They refuse to believe that actions have consequences.

There is no objective standard of right and wrong. Each makes his own rules as he goes along. *Moral relativism has become the "in thing".* With everybody making up his own rules for playing the game of life without a *"rule book"* or *"umpires".* It's no wonder confusion reigns.

The famed Psychiatrist, Dr. Karl Menninger, of the world-renowned Menninger Clinic, has been proclaimed the world's greatest psychiatrist. Dr. Menninger died a few years ago at 97 years of age. After years of successful treatment of mentally ill and emotionally disturbed patients, he wrote a book entitled, *"What Ever Happened to Sin."* In it he says, *"Sin really does exist."* He was distressed that modern society tries to figure out its problems and talk about morality without ever mentioning the word *"sin".* He was convinced that the *only way to raise the moral tone of present-day civilization and deal with the depression and anxieties that plague modern man, is to admit that there is right and wrong, virtue and "sin".*

With a degree in Psychology and more than 30 years of clinical practice as a Family Therapist, working with hurting people, I certainly do not reject psychology. But I *vehemently* reject any psychology or therapy that has no room nor need for God. The God who made us knows what makes us tick and has provided a book of instructions, the Bible. *When all else fails, it only makes sense to read the directions.*

We may prefer to call sin a mistake, a sickness, or a stumbling upward, but the Bible says, *"All have SINNED and come short of the glory of God."* (Rom. 3:23). It says, *"The heart is deceitful above all things and desperately wicked."* (Jer. 17:9) It says, *"If we say that we have no sin, we deceive ourselves, and the truth is not in us."* (I Jn. 1:8)

When God enscribed with His own hand upon tablets of stone, He did not write the *"Ten Suggestions"* but the *"Ten Commandments".* And when we murder, steal, lie, commit adultery, or bow down to worship ourselves, instead of God, it is rebellion against God and we *ought* to feel guilty.

The only true and lasting cure for sin and guilt is not found on a couch in some therapists office, but in Christ. Because of Christ's death upon the cross to pay the penalty for our sin, *"If we confess our sins, he is faithful and just to forgive us our sins, and to cleanse us from all unrighteousness."* (1 Jn. 1:9) And, *"though your sins be as scarlet, they shall be as white as snow; though they be red like crimson, they shall be as wool."* (Isaiah 1:18)

In 1966, B. J. Thomas' version of the famous Hank Williams song,"I'm So Lonesome I Could Cry," sold a million records. Then a concert tour with Gene Pitney's Cavalcade of Stars extended B. J.'s reputation. His song, "Raindrops Keep Fallin' on My Head" leaped to the. top of the charts in 1969—followed by a string of top ten records. Eventually, B. J. won five Grammy awards sold more than thirty-two million records and had an annual income of twelve million dollars.

The glitter and the acclaim, however, were only part of the story. B. J. Thomas, the recording star so admired by millions, remained in his own eyes the inadequate little boy who was never able to attract the love and approval of the only fan that really mattered to him—his Dad.

"When you're six years old and your dad says for the hundredth time, 'You dirty, shiftless, worthless bum, get out of here!', you believe it. You say to yourself, 'Man, I'm a dirty bum, and my dad wants me to get out.' I knew I was no good. Why? My idol, my father didn't like me."

B. J.'s dad, Vernon Thomas—always dictatorial and emotionally remote—had been raised by a father who operated a corn liquor still in the woods around Corsicana, Texas. Vernon was an alcoholic by age thirteen and known as "the biggest hell raiser in town." As a result B. J.'s childhood in Houston, Texas, was one frustrating scramble after another to win his father's love and approval. B. J. can remember breaking a glass or falling down to hurt himself—anything that would cause his dad to notice him. "I really wanted Dad to love me,' he recalls, "but other than a few yells or a slap on the side of the face, Dad never did seem to respond."

Predictably, the effect of the psychological abuse was negative, yet ultimately paradoxical. B. J. was highly motivated to prove that he could be successful. But as one success piled upon another, his low sense of self-esteem kept him from accepting those achievements. He was miserable.

Inevitably, strains developed in B. J.'s life. Although earning big bucks, he was in personal trouble. He and his wife, Gloria, separated. He knew that only a miracle could end the spiraling cycle of financial problems, drugs, alcohol and fuzzy thinking that hounded him. But a miracle—the first of many—happened.

A very sensitive and loving Christian couple stepped into Gloria's life. They listened as she unloaded on them her problems, and helped in every way they could. Within a few weeks Gloria experienced the miracle of Christian rebirth. She was changed, and with the help of these same friends, B.J. also discovered a personal walk with Jesus Christ. For the first time, he had the assurance that he was important—ultimately important—to God, his Heavenly Father.

"It finally dawned on me that God made me like anyone else, that Jesus Christ showed the way for me like anyone else," he recalls. "Suddenly a light bulb came on. I had a different feeling about myself. I didn't hate myself. I wanted to live. Before, I had always wanted to do better, but really deep down I felt like I was still that same kid my dad had taught me was no good."

Charles Colson, at age forty had become one of President Nixon's closest confidants He was known as the White House *"hatchet man"*—an ex-Marine Captain—who supposedly boasted that he would run over his own grandmother to reelect the President. Then, came watergate and seven months imprisonment for his part in that which brought down a President.

Colson began *Prison Fellowship* with a staff of six in 1976 and funded it with royalties from his best-selling book, *"Born Again"*. An independent research study, led by clinical psychologist, John Gartner, has concluded that, although the recidivism (*re-arrest*) rate of released prisoners is 75% (*most crimes are commited by repeat offenders*), those, receiving Christ through the ministry of Prison Fellowship and such ministries is *"phenomenally"* lower. In Brazil, for example, only 4% return to prison for repeat crimes.

What was it that transformed Chuck Colson from a *"hatchet man"* who was so consumed with a desire for power that he would *"run over his own grandmother"*? What was it that so dramatically changed a *"tough, wily, nasty"* ex-Marine Captain who was convicted and imprisoned for his part in Watergate? He was *"born again"*. As he relates in his book, *"Born Again"*, he experienced a personal relationship with Jesus Christ.

One night, when he was in the throes of crippling anxiety and debilitating depression as a result of the Watergate trials, he visited an old friend, Tom Philips. Tom was president of the Raytheon Corp., where by hard work he had reached the pinacle of worldly success at age 40. Yet, he told Chuck that he felt a terrible emptiness. He would get up in the middle of the night and just stare out the window. Life seemed to have no meaning.

Billy Graham was holding a crusade at Madison Square Garden in New York. Tom decided he would go out of curiosity. Billy's message seemed to speak specially to him. When the invitation was given, he found himself making his way down to the front. He testifies, *"That night I asked Jesus to come into my life and I could feel His presence with me, His peace within me. Everything was different. Something happened and I knew it."*

"Would you like to pray, Chuck?" Tom asked after telling of his experience. Chuck said, *"Yes"*. Colson relates, *"As Tom prayed, it sounded like he was speaking directly to God. Then there was a long silence. I knew he expected me to pray. But I just couldn't."*

Chuck excused himself, thanking Tom for his time and left. As he walked toward his car, his iron grip on his emotions began to relax, tears welled up in his eyes as he gropped for his keys in the darkness. He angrily brushed the tears away, but they just kept coming. *"What kind of weakness is this"?* he said to himself.

As he began to start the car, tears streaming down his cheeks, he knew that he had to go back and pray with Tom. But then, as he got out of the car, he saw the lights in the house go out. They had gone to bed. *"Why hadn't I prayed when I had the chance?"* he thought He felt so alone—really alone.

He drove away, tears still flowing, uncontrollably. He couldn't see to drive. He pulled over to the side of the road, cupped his face in his hands and laid his head down on the steering wheel. He forgot about machismo, pretences, and fears of being weak. He prayed for God's forgiveness and for what Tom had.

Colson says, *"I began to feel the wonderful feeling of being released. I had a sensation that water, not only was running down my cheek, but surging through my whole body, cleansing my very soul. There in an instant, all alone with God, I found Christ as my personal Savior. I was born again."*

In 1993 Charles Colson was named the recipient of the *"Templeton Prize"* for Progress in Religion. The Templeton Prize was founded in 1972 to honor a living person who has advanced the world's understanding of God or spirituality. The Prize is valued at more than one million dollars and is the world's largest annual award. Previous winners include Mother Theresa (1973), Billy Graham (1982), and Alexander Solzhenitsyn (1983). The entire amount of the funds awarded was used for Colson's Prison Fellowship Ministry, particularly among prisoners' families.

Not only do the decisions we make have consequences in this life, they have consequences through eternity.

Blaise Pascal, a French philosopher and mathematician, developed the science of probability and statistics, considered so essential to modern day science. He was miraculously converted from agnosticism to Christianity when he had a personal encounter with Jesus and was born again.

He was once asked by one of his associates in the scientific community, who was a skeptic, why he believed in life after death and the need for salvation in Christ. He replied, *"Let's assume that I am wrong and there is no life hereafter—then I have lost nothing. On the other hand, let's assume that I am right and there is life hereafter, then I have gained everything."*

CHAPTER 34

WHATEVER HAPPENED TO AMERICA'S SCHOOLS?

Standing before a huge American flag, Barbara Walters looked sternly into the television camera. *"The alarm has sounded,"* she said. *"The clock is ticking. But most of us are still asleep."* Nuclear threat? Acid rain? An epidemic?

No, Walters was referring to the deterioration of American education. *"Test scores are plummeting,"* she said. Most high school students she surveyed thought the Holocaust was a *"Jewish holiday."* Many couldn't locate the United States on a world map.

But Walters probed beyond academic performance. The real crisis, she argued, is one of character. *"Today's high school seniors live in a world of misplaced values,"* she said. *"They have no sense of discipline. No goals. They care only for themselves. In short, they are becoming a generation of undisciplined cultural barbarians."*

According to the National Education Association, the most frequent discipline problems in the public schools in the 1940s were talking, chewing gum, making noise, running in the halls, and violating the dress code. In the 1980s the most frequent discipline problems were drugs, alcohol, rape, robbery, and assault.

Today, kids are killing kids and their teachers. Metal detectors are necessary to try to keep out the guns and other deadly weapons. Gang warfare among even elementary age children is making our city streets and schools killing fields. Disillusioned teenagers are committing suicide as never before in history. More than fifty percent of the major crimes in America are committed by those under 18 years of age.

The one man that has had the most profound influence on modern public education was John Dewey. John Dewey was the father of so-called *"progressive education"* and the first president of the *"American Humanist Association"*. Like the Communists who set forth the *Communist Manifesto*, there is a *Humanist Manifesto*, and there is little difference in them.

John Dewey was one of the original 34 who drafted and signed the Humanist Manifesto. In summary it asserted: *that the universe was self-existing and not created; that man is a result of a continuous natural process; that mind is a projection of body and nothing more; that man is molded mostly by his culture; that there is no supernatural; that man has outgrown religion and any idea of God; that man's goal is the development of his own personality, which ceases to exist at death; that man will continue to develop to the point where he will look within himself and to the natural world for the solution to all of his problems; that all institutions and/or religions that in some way impede this "human development" must be changed; that socialism. is the ideal form of economics; and that all of mankind deserves to share in the fruits from following the above tenets.*

Concerning religion in particular it states, *"Though we consider the religious forms and ideas of our fathers no longer adequate, the quest for the good life is still the central task for mankind. Man is at last becoming aware that he alone is responsible for the realization of the world of his dreams, that he has within himself the power for its achievement...*

"We find insufficient evidence for belief in the existence of a supernatural; it is either meaningless or irrelevant to the question of the survival and fulfillment of the human race...Promises of immortal salvation or fear of eternal damnation are both illusory and harmful. They distract humans from present concerns, from self actualization and from rectifying social injustices. Modern science discredits such historic concepts as the "ghost in the machine" and the "separable soul."

John Dewy was also one of the founders of the ACLU along with Roger Baldwin. He believed in the philosophy of *"legal realism"* which is the belief that the courts should play an active role in the *making* of the law, not the legislature alone.

In a booklet entitled *"Schooling for the Future"*, Dr. John Goodman of the NEA states: *"Our goal is behavioral change. The majority of our youth still hold to the values of their parents."* (How terrible!!) He goes on to say, *"If we do not resocialize them to accept change our society may decay."*

"Atheistic secular humanism" has become the established religion of America through the control of the public schools by the high priests of Public Education. The ACLU is their legal enforcers.

One day I was handed a dollar bill that had been defaced by someone who had stamped in large red letters under the words, "IN GOD WE TRUST", the words, "THERE IS NO GOD TO TRUST." It was one of a number of such bills being circulated.

At first it made me extremely angry, that someone would dare to ridicule the faith of America's founding fathers and 94 per cent of Americans today, who, according to Gallup, believe *there is a God to trust*. But my anger turned to pity and concern for one, who is trying so desperately to deny, by *whistling in the dark,* that there is a God to be accountable to.

America's founding fathers *knew* that you could *not have* a free people very long *without* Biblical morality.

John Adams wrote, *"Our Constitution was made only for a moral and religious people. It is wholly inadequate to the government of any other."*

In his book, *"My Life Without God"*, William Murray, son of atheist, Madalyn Murray O'Hair and the plaintiff of record in the 1963 Supreme Court case banning prayer in the schools, describes his childhood years as a seedbed of violence, vindictiveness, and illusions of grandeur. He describes his mother's political involvement with the Communist Party along with the use of drugs and the smuggling of drugs from Mexico.

Because of her Marxist beliefs, Madalyn had sought to renounce her U. S. citizenship and become a citizen of Russia. Russia *wouldn't accept her*, however, because of her *inability* to *hold a job* for any length of time in the U. S. She was told to go back and work for a Communist revolution in America. She followed their instructions. Although she repeatedly denied being a Communist, she chaired the Baltimore chapter of the Communist organ, *Fair Play for Cuba*. (*Lee Harvey Oswald, who assassinated President Kennedy, was a member of the New Orleans chapter of Fair Play for Cuba.*) When the Communist party opened a book-store in Baltimore, Madalyn was asked to run it. Members of the Communist party frequently met at her house.

When Madalyn returned to the U. S., she was determined to remove religion from American society as a necessary, *preparatory step* for a Communist takeover. The Soviet system of suppressing religion no doubt showed her the way. The Soviets, through the courts, had criminalized any public expression of religion, except at a time and place sanctioned by the State. Even the home did not have religious freedom—*teaching one's children to believe in God was a crime.*

Judge Pendergast of the Baltimore Superior Court ruled in reference to the case to take prayer out of the schools: *"It is abundantly clear that the petitioner's real objective is to drive every concept of religion out of the public school system. If God were removed from the classroom, there would remain only atheism. Thus the beliefs of virtually all the pupils would be subordinated to those of Madalyn Murray."*

What was the prayer that was *so vile* and *offensive* that we *dare not* allow America's children with their impressionable minds hear, much less repeat? *"We thank you for the flowers so sweet; We thank you for the food we eat; We thank you for the birds that sing; We thank you God for everything."* So flushed with victory was Madalyn after winning her case, she filed suit against both the Pope and Billy Graham.

Finally, completely disillusioned with the emptiness of atheism, William Murray *rejected* all connections with the American

Atheists in 1977. He began to search for purpose and meaning in life. He was in San Francisco, Jan.24,1980, when awakening in the middle of the night, he felt compelled to read the Bible. He drove to a store on Fisherman's Wharf, where under a stack of *porno magazines* he found a Bible. In his room that night he *received* the *Person of the Book, JesusChrist,* as his personal Savior.

In a moment he found the peace and inner satisfaction he had been looking for, for 33 years. Although he had *tried everything else,* only now was he freed from the chains of alcoholism and even a three-pack-a-day cigarette habit. I have had the privilege of meeting and talking with William Murray. *He is definitely for real.*

May 10, 1980, William Murray wrote a letter of apology that appeared in the Baltimore Sun. It read: *"...I would like to apologize to the people...for whatever part I played in the removal of Bible reading and praying from the public schools... I now realize the value of this great tradition and importance it has played in the past in keeping America a moral and lawful country. I can now see the damage this removal has caused to our nation in the form of loss of faith and MORAL DECLINE..."*

Daniel Webster said some 200 years ago, almost as a prophecy, *"If we abide by the PRINCIPLES TAUGHT IN THE BIBLE, our country will go on prospering and to prosper, but if we and our posterity neglect its instructions and authority, no man can tell how sudden a catastrophe may overwhelm us and bury our glory in profound obscurity."*

Perhaps it is time we went back to that which worked: *The education started by America's founding fathers. It taught Johny how to read and that there was a difference between right and wrong.*

In 1983, Alexander Solzhenitsyn, winner of the 1970 Nobel Prize for Literature, gave an address in London in which he attempted to explain why so much evil had befallen his people, the Russians. He said:

"Over a half century ago, while I was still a child, I recall hearing a number of old people offer the following explanation for the great disasters that had befallen Russia: 'Men have forgotten God; that's why all this has happened.'

"Since then I have spent well-nigh 50 years working on the history of our revolution; in the process I have read hundreds of books, collected hundreds of personal testimonies, and have already contributed eight volumes of my own toward the effort of clearing away the rubble left by that upheaval.

"But if I were asked today to formulate as concisely as possible the main cause of the ruinous revolution that swallowed up some 60 million of our people, I could not put it more accurately than to repeat: 'Men have forgotten God, that's why all this has happened.'"

Among the dramatic changes that occurred with the fall of Communism in the Soviet Union was an openness to explore spiritual matters. Although banned for 70 years since the Revolution, the Bible is fast becoming the most popular book in Russia and other formerly atheist countries.

Dr. Michail Matskovsky, a Russian social scientist, and a member of the Russian Academy of Sciences, visited America. Dr. Matskovsky stated that Russian schools have recently added Scripture and religion courses to their curriculum.

Why the sudden change of heart from an avowedly atheistic nation? With the near collapse of the communist economy, government leaders are willing to explore societies that have endured. America was the first democracy and has endured for over 200 years.

Dr. Matskovsky believes the strength of America's system lies in its Judeo-Christian values, which are based upon the Ten Commandments. He came to America to observe this Christian value system firsthand.

The most remarkable thing he witnessed was our respect for life. One example he noted was, *"the privileged parking spaces we reserve for the disabled"*. *"You would never see that in my country,"* he commented. It is rather, *"Survival of the Fittest"*; let the weak be damned. Biblical Christianity, however, emphasizes the dignity and infinite value of every individual.

Another Russian scientist, Dr. Dmitry A. Kuznetsov, also visited the U. S. Dr. Kuznetsov is a world renowned biochemist and winner of the prestigious Lenin Komsomol Prize in Science, an award given annually to Russia's two brightest young scientists. He holds three earned doctorates: an M.D. in internal Diseases, a Ph.D. in Biochemistry, and a D.Sc. in Molecular Biology.

While working in Moscow in the 1980's, Dr. Kuznetsov came to the conclusion that the theory of evolution, that he had been force-fed as *"fact"* from early childhood, was the cruelest hoax ever to be perpertrated on mankind.

The more he learned of science, the more he realized that the supposed *"scientific evidences"* for evolution were based entirely on unprovable assumptions. He came to the conclusion that the fathomless intricacies of design he saw in everything his scientifically trained eye observed, demanded an intelligent Creator and Designer. Without ever having read or being exposed to the Bible, he became a *"scientific creationist"*. He turned from atheism to a belief in God.

Dr. Kuznetsov subsequently joined the Moscow Baptist Church and is currently writing a column, *"Science Without Atheism"* for an independent newspaper with a rapidly growing circulation in Russia.

While in the United States, Dr. Kuznetsov lectured at a number of American Universities, including Yale and U.C.L.A. Dr. Kuznetsov noted the irony that, *"It seems that scientists have more academic freedom these days in Moscow than they do in America where only evolution can be taught as science in the public schools."*

Sociologists at the University of California, Berkeley, conducted a six year study of middle-class Americans and noted the difference between two value systems. They first noted the *"biblical view"*, which asserts the dignity of an individual, who is created by God. It, therefore, follows that no one is to be casually sacrificed.

Community service and concern for the weak and defenseless

is emphasized. But the Berkeley sociologists concluded that the "*biblical*" value system is giving way to "*individualism,*" a system where "*I*" am only concerned about "*my*" rights, "*my*" advancement and "*my*" pursuit of happiness. Whatever makes "*me*" happy is what's important. Isn't it a fascinating paradox that while Russian children are studying Bibles in their classrooms, the Bible is banned in America's classrooms lest America's kids be "*polluted*" with Judeo-Christian values.

"*This know, also, that in the last days perilous times shall come. For men shall be lovers of their own selves, covetous, boasters, proud, blasphemers, disobedient to parents, unthankful, unholy, Without natural affection, trucebreakers, false accusers, incontinent, fierce, despisers of those that are good, Traitors, heady, high-minded, lovers of pleasures more than lovers of God.*" (2 Tim. 3:1-4) "*Professing themselves to be wise, they become fools.. Who exchange the truth of God for a lie, and worship and serve the creature more than the Creator...*" (Rom. l:22-25)

Although recent Gallup polls indicate that 94% of Americans believe there is a God and 77% believe that voluntary prayer and Bible reading without commentary or proselytizing should be permitted in the public schools, we have allowed a very small but vocal minority to play the censor.

CHAPTER 35

WHATEVER HAPPENED TO THE FAMILY?

A couple that had been married for many years were lying in bed just before drifting off to sleep. The wife's thoughts began to drift back through the years and she jarred her busband awake with the words, *"Honey, do you remember how you used to whisper sweet nothings in my ear before we went to sleep?"* The husband stirred himself awake, turned over and whispered all the *"sweet nothings"* he could think of for the moment and again settled down to sleep.

Just about the time he drifted off again, she whispered in her most sultry voice, *"Honey do you remember how passionately you used to kiss me before we went to sleep"*. Again, he turned over and planted a loving, lingering kiss upon her lips.

He was again drifting off when he heard her say, *"Honey, do you remember how you used to bite me affectionately on the ear?"*

He jumped out of bed. There was a crash, and a yell of pain. "Honey, what's the mat ter?" "Oh, I fell over a chair...I was going after my teeth."

Keeping the romance alive and having a happy, successful, fulfilling marriage is not something that just happens. It is something that has to be worked at, even if it hurts sometimes.

When God created the heavens and the earth, including Adam, He looked at His handiwork and pronounced it good. But then He saw Adam in his loneliness, and said, *"It isn't good for man to be alone; I will make a companion for him, a helper suited to his needs.. Then the Lord God caused the man to fall into a deep sleep, and took one of his ribs and closed up the place from which he had removed it, and made the rib into a woman and brought her unto the man."* (Gen. 2:18,21,22 TLB)

Perhaps the women would prefer the slightly altered rendition of the story by a little girl. When asked to describe the creation of man, she said, *"God reached down his hands, picked up some modeling clay, and made a man. When he looked at man, he said, `I think I can do better than that if I tried again. So then he created woman!"*

Why did God use a rib with which to make woman? According to Jewish tradition, God made woman not from man's head to lord over him, nor from his feet to be trampled under by him, but from his side to be equal to him, from under his arm to be protected by him and from near his heart to be loved by him.

If ever there was a couple whose marriage was made in heaven, and made for one another, it was Adam and Eve. There was no one around to complain, *"I don't know what the younger generation is coming to."* There were no in-law problems. Adam did not have to listen to Eve describe all of the other men she could have married. Nor did Eve have to endure Adam's comparison of her cooking to the way his mother cooked.

They didn't have to worry about finances, for God placed them in a beautiful garden, and provided ample food for them to eat. They didn't need clothes nor shelter, for it was a paradise. But something went dreadfully wrong. They chose to believe the lies of Satan rather than obey God and partook of the fruit of the only tree in all the garden forbidden to them.

Adam and Eve sinned, not by having sex, as some claim, but by chosing to disobey God's commandments. God had already blessed them and told them, *"Multiply and fill the earth and subdue it..."* (Gen. 1:28) There is only one way to multiply—and God blessed it.

Why did things go wrong? Because they refused to believe that God's will was best. They like so many, chose to ignore God and do their own thing, their way. They removed God from the center place in their lives and in their marriage.

As old-fashioned as that may seem to some, the presence of

God does make a difference in the home. In the family where both the husband and wife are Christians, where they read the Bible and pray daily, where they attend church together and seek God's will when they make decisions—there is a uniting force which is absent in marriages where God is ignored.

Notice how, after Adam and Eve sinned, suffering the consequences, they each sought to blame the other. Adam blamed Eve and even God. He said, *"The woman whom Thou gavest to be with me, she gave me from the tree, and I ate."* (Gen. 3:12)

Poor Adam, what could he do? If he had refused Eve's offer, he probably would have never heard the end of it! God should have known better than to give him such a woman! Eve blamed the serpent (Satan). Neither wanted to accept responsibility for their decisions and actions. It was someone else's fault that they had problems.

From the beginning of mankind, God intended that man and woman be joined together into a lasting union (Gen. 2:24). God made only one Eve as a help-meet for Adam. He could have made several Eves for Adam just in case the first relationship didn't work out, but Adam just had so many ribs.

They had problems with their children, too. Their first born, Cain, murdered his brother Abel in a jealous rage. In spite of all their problems they managed to stay together as husband and wife for 800 or 900 years give or take a few. I would consider that a pretty stable marriage.

Surely those of us who have managed, by the grace of God, to escape the tragedy of divorce, dare not look down our pharasaical noses at those who haven't. Jesus said to those that were about to stone the woman caught in adultery, *"Let him that is without sin cast the first stone."* (John 8:1-11) The Bible says, *"God hates divorce."* (Mal. 2:16). Why? Because divorce hurts. It hurts the couple involved, the children, and society. Those who have suffered through a divorce need our sympathy and support, not condemnation.

You would think that after 6,000 years of practice men and women would have learned how to get along with one another.

Twenty percent of all police officers killed in the line of duty are killed while answering calls involving family fights Approximately twelve to fifteen million wives are battered each year.

A wife was overheard saying to her husband, *"I know you believe you understand what you think I said, but I'm not sure you realize that what you think you heard is not what I meant."*

In the classified ad section of a small-town newspaper, the following ad appeared on Monday:

"FOR SALE: R. D. Jones has one sewing machine for sale. Phone 958 after 7 p.m. and ask for Mrs. Kelly who lives with him cheap.

On Tuesday: NOTICE: We regret having erred in R. D. Jones' ad yesterday. It should have read: One sewing machine for sale. Cheap. Phone 958 and ask for Mrs. Kelly who lives with him after 7 p.m.

On Wednesday: R. D. Jones has informed us that he has received several annoying telephone calls because of the error we made in his classified ad yesterday. His ad stands corrected as follows: FOR SALE: R. D. Jones has one sewing machine for sale. Cheap. Phone 958 after 7 p.m. and ask for Mrs. Kelly who loves with him.

Finally on Thursday: NOTICE: I, R.D. Jones have no sewing machine for sale. I smashed it. Don't call 958 as the telephone has been taken out. I have not been carrying on with Mrs. Kelly. Until yesterday she was my housekeeper, but she quit."

As you can see, correct communication is important. You cannot have a good relationship with others without good communication. Communication is the process of sharing yourself verbally and nonverbally that the other person can both accept and understand what you are sharing. But that is only half of good communication. The other half is listening.

Of all the psychological needs of man, the greatest of all is to be loved and to love. And that love must be communicated. Jesus said, *"A new commandment I give unto you, that ye love one another; as I have loved you."* (John 13:34) He didn't say TRY to love one another if the feeling comes, and they are loveable and attractive. It was a COMMAND. Love is an act of the will, not a chemical reaction. It is a psychological principle that if we act the way we want to feel, we will soon feel the way we act. LOVE is a CHOICE.

Love is defined as *"seeking the best for the one loved."* But not only is love good for the one loved, it is good for the one who loves. A certain insurance company found in a statistical survey that men who hug and kiss their wives every morning before leaving for work, live five years longer than the average.

The famous dietician, Dr. Carlton Fredericks, was once asked to explain the relationship between love and nutrition. He said, *"When a fellow kisses a girl, the adrenosympathetic system calls on the liver for glycogen for energy. This in turn forces the release of insulin, vitamin B-l, and phosphorus to burn the sugar. In his brain, if he is doing any thinking, which is problematical, there is an exchange of starch, phosphorus, and thiamine between the thalamic and the cortical brain. As the pulse and respiration rates rise, there is increased exchange of oxygen on the intracellular level, which would mean increased consumption of thiamine and phosphorus."* I think he was saying, *"Love is good for you."*

Anthropologist, George Murdock, who analyzed some 500 cultures, found only one society that lacked the basic family unit as we know it, and it is extinct!

He writes, *"Among the Nayars paternity was apparently a one night thing, offspring being reared by the mother and her female relatives. The actual father of the child was usually not known, since the mother willingly accepted passing visitors as sexual partners. Since the 'visiting husbands' came only at night, the relationships hardly involved either a marriage or a common residence."* No wonder they became extinct!

Divorce and single parenthood in America is reaching epidemic proportions. Almost half of the marriages begun each year end in divorce before the fifth anniversary. In the high population areas the number of divorces granted annually exceeds the number of marriages performed. Recent studies indicate that almost half of

America's children live apart from their natural fathers, and millions of children are growing up in homes without a male role model.

These are far more likely to live below the poverty line, drop out of school, engage in drug and alcohol use, commit criminal acts, and score lower on tests. Out of one thousand girls in a Pennsylvania reform school, only 87 came from homes in which there was a traditional husband wife relationship. More than nine hundred were from broken homes.

According to Paul Peterson of the Brookings Institute, *"The most powerful force contributing to the formation of the urban underclass, perversely enough, may be the changing value in American society, in which the virtues of family stability, mutual support, and religious based commitment to the marriage vow no longer command the deference they once did."*

Some thirty years ago, Harvard sociologist, Pitirim Sorokin, predicted, *"Divorces and separations will increase until any profound difference between socially sanctioned marriage and illicit sex-relationship disappears.... The main sociocultural functions of the family will further decrease until the family becomes a mere incidental cohabitation of male and female, while the home will be an overnight parking place."* Not only has his prophecy come true, but we are reaping the consequences.

For more than 200 years, almost without exception, Americans have held steadfastly to the Judeo-Christian concept of the family based on the Bible. Even Hollywood and the media promoted this ideal with such shows as *"Father Knows Best", "Ozzie and Harriet"* and *"Leave it to Beaver".* We look back on those days as *"Happy Days".*

At the *"Little Brown Church"* near Nashua, Iowa, the pastor has a unique way of communicating to the couples he marries, the need for each to accept their own responsibility for the success of the marriage.

After the ceremony, he walks with the couple to the entrance of the church and says, *"Before you go, the bride has the honor of ringing the bell."* However, the bell is so heavy that she cannot ring it by herself. The minister says to the groom, *"Lend a hand."* Together they pull and the bell rings. Then the minister says to the couple, *"Never forget that as long as you pull together you can ring the bell."*

Ted Koppel of *"Nightline"* in a commencement address at Duke University said, *"We have actually convinced ourselves that slogans will save us. 'Shoot up if you must; but use a clean needle.' Enjoy sex, whenever and with whomever you wish; but wear a condom.' What Moses brought down from Mount Sinai were not the Ten Suggestions. They are Commandments. There is harmony and inner peace to be found in following a moral compass that points in the same direction, regardless of fashion or trend."*

In 1874, Mr. and Mrs. Danks, with their little brood of children, were a happy and devoted couple. Both were in their early thirties.

Mr. Danks was a song writer of growing reputation. The couple had beautiful dreams of going down life's pathway and growing old together. In the atmosphere of this joyous anticipation, he wrote one of the most popular love songs ever written, *"Silver Threads among the Gold."* Mr. Danks dedicated it to his wife.

But, marital discord came into the Dank's household. Separation followed! When Mr. Danks died in 1903, He was found dead, kneeling beside his bed. On an old copy of the famous song, he had written these words: *"It's hard to grow old alone!"*

William and Mary Tanner were crossing a railroad track when Mary's foot slipped and became wedged between the rail and a wooden crosswalk. Frantically she tried to get loose as a train approached around the curve. Her husband attempted to free her. As the express came closer with its brakes screeching, Mary realized it couldn't stop in time. *"Leave me, Bill! Leave me!"* she cried.

Seeing his efforts were useless, he arose quickly and held her in his arms to protect her as much as possible. While bystanders shuddered in horror, the train thundered over them. It was reported that just before the engine hit them, they heard the man cry, *"I'll stay with you, Mary!"*

A young couple was visiting with an older couple celebrating their 50th anniversary. *"Fifty years!"* one of them exclaimed. *"That's a long time to be married to one person."* The old gentleman looked over at his wife with love in his eyes and said, *"It would have been a lot longer without her."*

Having reached the milestone of 57 years married to the same woman, I can, wholeheartedly, say *"Amen"* to the *"old gentleman's"* statement, *"It would have at least seemed a lot longer without the helpmeet God gave me."*

CHAPTER 36

SATISFACTION GUARANTEED, NOW & FOREVER

Dale Evans Rogers grew up in a Christian home with a mother and a father that told her about Jesus as soon as she was able to understand. They took her to Sunday School and church from the time she was a babe in arms. When she was ten years of age, Dale accepted Christ as her personal Saviour during a revival meeting.

She testifies, however, that although she received Jesus as her Saviour, she did not surrender her will to Him. Her number one goal in life was to be a success in the business and entertainment world. She eloped with her first sweetheart while still in her early teens. From this union was born her son, Tom. Dale says, *"Although my first marriage was a failure, my son was not."*

At 28, she wound up in Hollywood under contract to a movie studio. Although she began to acquire fame and fortune and the things, that should have made her happy, she was miserable. She was now married to Roy Rogers, the *"King of the Cowboys,"* but life was full of disillusionment, insecurity, and disappointment.

Seeking answers, she attended church one Sunday evening with her son, Tom. During the service, he turned to her and asked, *"Mother, is everything alright between you and the Lord"* Dale hastily explained that she had accepted Christ when she was 10. *"But Mother,"* Tom urged, *"you don't know Christ the way I do! If you did, you wouldn't be so restless, always searching for some new kind of reli-*

gion to give you peace of mind." With tears in his eyes, he pleaded, "*Jesus is all you need!*"

Dale crumbled inside, and she testifies, "*Suddenly the falsity and emptiness of my existence loomed up before me. I knew why I had made such a mess of things: I had never surrendered my will to Christ.*" God continued to deal with her during the following week.

She could hardly wait for the next Sunday and when Dr. Jack MacArthur gave the invitation, Dale says, "*I raced down the aisle of that First Baptist Church of Eagle Rock and found peace and joy in the prayer room as I came clean with God and turned my life over to him.*"

She says, "*I walked out of that church with a song springing up in my heart and a brand new perspective on* life." Dale not only had peace with God, but "*the peace of God, which passeth all understanding.*" (Phil. 4:7)

Seeing the change in Dale, Roy began attending church. Roy testifies, "*I had been brought up in a God fearing home, but like an awful lot of youngsters, I sort of drifted away from church-going, and even from thinking much about religion. With Dale's help, I started catching that same feeling I'd noticed in her. The day came when I, too, accepted Christ as my personal Saviour and joined the church along with her.*"

Roy and Dale Rogers, have been an inspiration to millions by their public stand for Christian principles and values. In this day when America's traditional values based on the Bible are under attack, our young people, especially, need to know that there are those in the public eye that still hold to those values.

God has promised "*Happy Trails*" for those that trust in His Son, Jesus Christ, and seek to do His will. The storms of life may bear down upon us, the trail may seem steep at times, but God has promised that He will be with us, through it all. "*And we know that all things work together for good to them that love God, to them who are the called according to his purpose.*" (Rom. 8:28)

More than ever, however, the American dream seems to be life, liberty, and the *purchase* of happiness. When elections come around, it seems that most Americans vote their *pocketbooks* above all else.

Though we may deny it, materialism has become for too many their *"god"*.

In 1991, 74 percent of Americans entering college declared that their most important life goal was *"becoming very well off financially"*. Although many laughingly say, *"Money can't buy happiness"*, few really believe it.

As cultures become more affluent, do their people become happier? In 1957 America's per person income, expressed in today's dollars, was less than $8,000. Today, it is more than twice that. Compared to 1957, we have twice as many cars per person; we have microwave ovens, color TVs, VCRs, air conditioners, cell phones, computers and $12 billion a year worth of brand-name athletic shoes.

So, are we happier than we were 40 years ago? In 1957, 35 percent of Americans told the National Opinion Research Center, they were *"very happy."* In the 1990s, however, with doubled American affluence, only 31 percent said the same.

To judge by soaring rates of clinical depression, the quintupling of the violent crime rate since 1960, the doubling of the divorce rate, and the tripling of the teen suicide rate, it would seem that *"Money and the accumulation of things has not brought happiness."*

Many psychologists believe that today's epidemic levels of clinical depression stems from impoverished social connections. Today, 24 percent of Americans live alone, up from 8 percent a half-century ago. And half of America's children are being raised in single parent homes. The American Psychological Association recently rated *"the decline of the nuclear family"* as the number one *threat* to *mental health*. Teen-agers by the millions are joining gangs, looking for connectedness and family.

Cursed, rejected and abused by his parents in Puerto Rico, and completely on his own, as a 15 year old boy in the slums of New York City; Nicky Cruz became part of a vicious street gang and their leader. Violence, drugs, alcohol and crime was a way of life. Hatred of others, especially the police and those in authority, seethed within. Then one day he met a preacher, Dave Wilkerson, who told him that Jesus loved him and even though Nicky cursed him and knocked him down, said he loved him too.

Dave Wilkerson was holding meetings at a local theatre and invited Nicky and his gang of hoodlums, the Mau Maus, to attend. Nicky laughed at the whole idea, but thought it would be great fun to go and mock and disrupt the services.

So, 75 Mau Mau's and their girlfriends attended. With jeers, and cat calls, they succeeded in driving the young lady singer off the stage in tears. For about 15 minutes Wilkerson preached abont Jesus' love for them in spite of their sins, and gave an invitation to receive forgiveness for their sins and Christ as their Savior. When Nicky looked up he saw that the preacher was weeping, his lips trembling, as he prayed for them.

Nicky says, *"I knew that that preacher had something, I didn't have and that he was in the very presence of Jesus Christ, his friend and savior. I felt crushed by my sins and I began crying in repentance for my sins. It was the first time I had shed a tear since I was 8 years old and my mother cursed me and threw me out..*

Before I knew it, I was on my knees at the front. There for the first time, I discovered two kinds of love—human and divine. When the two came together, something supernatural and heavenly happened to me. My eyes swam with tears and my chest burned with a pain so intense that I could only call out the name of 'Jesus'."

"I was born again. Delivered! Released! I was delirious with this feeling of divine love. I was loved—by the Almighty Creator of the Universe! My conflict and loneliness and guilt were replaced with the most incredible sense of peace and forgiveness and bubbling, irrepressible joy!"

God's presence was so profound in that meeting, that a great number of the Mau Mau's and other gang members received Christ, too. Wilkerson gave each of them a Bible. There was such a change in their lives and attitudes that the next week, with their Bible in one hand and their guns and knives in the other, they marched into the local police station and laid their weapons on the desk.

They then asked the "cops", their former enemies, who were standing in open-mouthed amazement and unbelief, to autograph their Bibles.

So dramatic was the change in the lives of these former hoodlums, that a major motion picture was produced, "*The Cross and the Switchblade*", portraying this remarkable account of the power of Christ's love to change lives. Eric Estrada of "*Chips*" fame, played the part of Nicky Cruz and Pat Boone, Dave Wilkerson.

Out of this grew what has proven itself through many years of ministry, to be one of the most effective programs ever, for rescuing and delivering teens and others from the chains of addiction to drugs, alcohol and involvement in gangs. It is called "*Teen Challenge*". Although it involves counseling and peer support groups, at its heart like many other "*Overcomer*" programs is the power of the love of Christ to change the individual.

What is the answer to societies problems? It is the miracle working power of God in the lives of individuals. Are religious people mentally and physically healthy? Or is religion a sign of neurosis, an ineffective coping mechanism employed by immature persons? Is religion, as Freud suggested, an illusion and guilt-producing obsessional neurosis? Or does religion, instead, contribute to one's well-being and happiness? Recent empirical studies would indicate that it does, especially to the strongly committed.

Psychiatrist, Dr. David Larson, Senior Researcher with the National Institute of Mental Health in Washington, D. C. states, *"During my training as a psychiatrist, I had been told repeatedly that religion was clinically harmful. I decided to investigate the psychiatric journals for empirical evidence to see if they supported the harmful effect of religion. I actually believed the evidence would indicate religion was harmful, but I found... the data showed instead that religion was highly beneficial—beneficial in more than 80 percent of the cases found in the psychiatric research."*

Dr. Larson found that church attendance, prayer, and the social support available in church were frequently found to be significant positive factors in helping patients with mental or physical health problems. It was observed empirically that faith in God increased dramatically an individual's ability to cope in a crisis. The studies showed that the religiously committed were far less likely to experience mental illness, drug abuse, alcoholism, and clinical depression.

First of all, the Christian life provides social support. Faithful churchgoers possess a sense of connectedness, of being upheld by the ties that bind, of bearing one another's burdens.

Second, religious faith gives people something worth living and dying for. An important ingredient of well-being is a sense of meaning and purpose.

Third, the Christian gospel offers unconditional acceptance. For those struggling with self-esteem, Christian faith offers good news: The universe has a Creator who became human to demonstrate unconditional love for each of us. No longer do we need to define our self-worth by our achievements, our possessions, or others' approval. We need only accept that we are accepted.

Fourth, Christian discipleship allows people to work for something bigger than themselves. Happy people are not those grasping for happiness, but those focused on things beyond themselves.

Most of all, committed Christians are happier because they have an eternal perspective. They can rest, confidently, in the hope that no matter how difficult things may be in this life, the Sovereign God they worship will one day make all things right. *"Godliness with contentment is great gain. For we brought nothing into this world and it is certain we can carry nothing out. And having food and raiment let us be therewith content." (1 Tim.6:6)*

Happiness is a choice. It is not the responsibility of others to make us happy, it is our responsibility to chose to work toward it (to pursue it). Life is fraught with troubles, difficulties and heartaches and there is no escaping it in this life. We need to pray the serenity prayer, *"God grant me the strength to change the things I can, The grace to accept the things I can't, And the wisdom to know the difference."*

Not only does Christ satisfy in life now, he satisfies for eternity. We don't like to think of death, but we all know that it is something we must face someday.

A woman had been diagnosed with a terminal illness and been given three months to live. So, as she was getting her things in order, she contacted her pastor and had him come to her house to discuss certain aspects of her final wishes. She told him which songs she wanted sung at the service, what scriptures she would like read, and what outfit she wanted to be buried in. The woman, also, requested to be buried with her favorite Bible. Everything was in order and the pastor was preparing to leave when the woman suddenly remembered something very important to her.

"*Ther's one more thing,*" she said excitedly. "*What's that?*" came the pastors reply. "*This is very important,*" the woman continued..."*I want to be buried with a fork in my right hand.*" The pastor stood looking at the woman, not knowing quite what to say.

"*That surprises you, doesn't it?*" the woman asked. "*Well, to be honest, I'm puzzled by the request,*" said the pastor. The woman explained, "*In all my years of attending church socials and potluck dinners, I always remember that when the dishes of the main course were being cleared, someone would inevitably lean over and say, 'keep your fork'. It was my favorite part, because I knew that something better was coming...like velvety chocolate cake or deep-dish apple pie. Something wonderful, and with substance! So, I just want people to see me there in that casket with a fork in my hand and I want them to wonder 'What's with the fork?' Then I want you to tell them: 'Keep Your Fork...The best is yet to come!'*"

The pastor's eyes welled up with tears of joy, as he hugged the woman goodbye. He knew this would be one of the last times he would see her before her death. But he also knew that the woman had a better grasp of heaven than he did. She KNEW that something better was coming.

At the funeral people were walking by the woman's casket and they saw the pretty dress she was wearing and her favorite Bible and fork placed in her right hand. Over and over the pastor heard the question, "*What's with the fork?*" And over and over he smiled.

During his message, the pastor told the people of the conversation he had with the woman shortly before she died. He also told them about the fork and about what it symbolized to her. The pastor told the people how he could not stop thinking about the fork, and told them that they probably would not be able to stop thinking about it either. He was right. "*The best is yet to come.*"

A little five-year-old boy lay dying of lung cancer in a Southern California hospital. His mother, a sweet Christian, came faithfully to comfort her child day after day. On Christmas eve the child's condition worsened. The nurses began to hear cries coming from his room. The sounds continued off and on throughout the night.

Christmas morning the mother arrived and asked how her son was doing. The nurses told her that he had begun hallucinating. They said that he kept saying something about bells ringing.

The mother abruptly halted her departure from the nurses' desk, turned, and spoke in an emphatic tone, *"Now you listen to me. My little boy isn't hallucinating. 'Cause you see, I told him when he gets to hurtin' real bad, so bad he can't stand it—if he'll just look up to Jesus, and listen real hard, he'll hear the bells of heaven ringin' for him. It'll be Jesus ringin' those bells, ready to welcome him home!"*

And with those words, the mother spun on her heels, and calmly walked down the hall and into her baby's room. There she lifted the child up, cradled him in her arms, settled back in a rocking chair, and gently began to stroke his small face.

They rocked and talked and rocked and talked about the *bells of heaven*, until the child gave a whisper-soft gasp and went to be with Jesus on Jesus' birthday.

In death, God will cradle His children in His loving arms, and *"wipe away all tears from our eyes, and there shall be no more death, neither sorrow, nor crying, neither shall there be any more pain: for the former things are passed away."* (Rev. 21:4)

A preacher was riding the train on his way to his next preaching assignment. A young man sat down beside him. He was fidgety and it was evident he was very nervous. The preacher asked him if something was troubling him and if he could help.

The young man began to pour out his story. He said, *"Five years ago, my father and I had a big fight, I hit him and stormed out of the house, cursing and swearing never to return.*

"I went to the city; got a job, and have had no contact with my parents for five years. A few weeks ago, after years of refusing to even think of home, I grew so homesick, I could hardly stand it. I wrote a letter home, telling my mom and dad that I would like to come home, but I didn't know if I'd be welcome."

He continued, *"The train passes by their farm and I told them, if I could come home, to tie a yellow ribbon on the old oak tree near the track. If it wasn't there, I would just stay on the train and ride on by."*

He said, *"We're almost there, and I can't bear to look. Would you look for me?"*

As they passed the farm, the preacher turned to the young man, whose eyes were moistening with tears, and the preacher with a thrill in his voice, shouted: *"Son, there's a yellow ribbon on every branch of that tree. Welcome home."*

On that day when we come to that place of many mansions, I believe there will be yellow ribbons on every branch of the *Tree of Life*, welcoming God's children home.

"...I will be SATISFIED, when I awake, with thy likeness." (Psalm 17:15)

Printed in the United States
30503LVS00004B/46